Let's
Quit
Kidding
Ourselves
About
Missions!

by
James M. Weber

MOODY PRESS

CHICAGO

ISBN: 0-8024-4678-7

Printed in the United States of America

To
Dr. R. S. Beal, Sr.,
for fifty-two years pastor of the First Baptist
Church of Tucson, Arizona. His example both in
and out of the pulpit had much to do with the
directing of two young minds toward "those
things which are above" (Col. 3:1).

Contents

Foreword

How long has it been since you read a book written by a missionary? That's probably the reason you should read this one. Missionaries see world missions differently from the way most of us see it, and we need at least to evaluate the situation from their perspective.

Jim Weber is not only a veteran of over twenty-five years on the field, but he also has a successful track record that qualifies him a hearing. He is no mystical idealist. He is a practical realist, and he communicates as one whether speaking or writing.

This book needs to be read by pastors, church members, young people, and certainly anyone planning to go to the mission field. Personally, I am planning to get one for every member of our church missionary board, for Jim has courageously shed light on some subjects that are very obscure to many in the church. I don't know of another book quite like it. Frankly, I didn't know Jim had such a sense of humor as comes through in his writing. That is particularly unusual in view of the fact that the subject is quite heavy—reaching the over 3 billion souls on planet earth who do not know Jesus Christ. Jim's sense of humor helps somewhat to soften the confrontation approach he gives to a problem we don't often like to face—what we have been calling "missions" is not true New Testament missions, for we have been kidding ourselves.

Any Christian will benefit from reading this book.

Tim LaHaye
Pastor, Scott Memorial Baptist Church
San Diego, California

Preface

The message of this book is not easy to write about, nor will it be very popular with many churchgoers today, but twenty-five years of experience on the foreign mission field have given me some ever growing convictions in relation to missions. One of those convictions is that the evangelical church in America in general, and many, many believers in particular, are deceived about this business of missions.

We know that the harvest is great and that the laborers are few, but somehow or other, the average evangelical Christian does not identify personally with that problem. *He may be aware of the problem, but he is not aware of the fact that he is part of the problem.* We have all heard the expression, "We can't see the forest for the trees," and the application is obvious. The best way to gain a perspective of a forest is not from down in, but from up on the nearby mountaintop or in an airplane.

Few men have really seen our planet, but those who have have traveled far to see it in perspective. In the same sense, the foreign missionary has opportunity to gain an overall view of the American church by virtue of time and distance. The changes that have come about so slowly are by and large unnoticed by many within the church, but one who has been away for a time sees those changes readily.

Evangelical Americans have long prided themselves on their missionary outreach. Schools, churches, and all kinds of Christian organizations know it is good P.R. to be on the side of missions, and the phrase "majoring in missions" is very popular. As a matter of fact, many churches want so desperately to convince themselves that they are missionary minded and that they are majoring in missions that those who prepare the budget end up placing everything possible under the heading of missions. If the church owns and operates a school, that is called missions. If the people at the church have a bus ministry, they call it missions. If they have a youth outreach during the week, it comes under missions in the budget. And when all these items are added up the people are quite well pleased with their "missions budget."

Please do not misunderstand what I am saying. In no way is it my intention to question the validity of Christian education. We need far more effort in this field. Your local church situation may well justify a bus ministry, and we praise the Lord for every church actively engaged in reaching children during the week. All I am saying is, let's keep our nomenclature straight. Let's call education just that—education. Let's call evangelism evangelism, and let's call missions missions. I grant you that the term *missions* has become one of many words in our English language which have come to mean everything in general and nothing in particular. And that suits the enemy of the church just fine: confusion always works to his advantage, because confusion produces complacency.

Of necessity I should start off by defining some terms and thus eliminating some of the confusion at the beginning of our consideration. We need to understand what we mean when we speak of missions and we need to know what it means to "major in missions."

When we look up the word *missions* or *missionary* in a dictionary, we discover a number of meanings, but basic to each one is the idea of sending or being sent. Actually, in a very loose sense, a boy sent to the store by his mother for a loaf of bread is on a mission and thus could be called a missionary. If one is willing to settle for that type of definition, I concede that the school and the buses and the youth work, and a good many other things, might logically be included in your "missions" budget. My contention, however, is that the terms *missions* and *missionary* in the scriptural sense allow for no such interpretation. Actually the terms are not even found in our English Bibles. The original thought from which we get the terms has to do with the sending of one or more believers for the expressed purpose of sharing the good news with another group of people. Distance is implied, as is the crossing of cultural lines, and it is my conviction that Scripture indicates that a special gift is involved. That is, just as the gift of teaching or preaching is considered a prerequisite for a pastoral ministry, so the missionary requires a gift. Some Bible scholars today equate the New Testament apostle with the present day missionary. Be that as it may, in this book I use the term *missions* in the following way:

> Missions is the business of sending out particular members of the body of Christ from any given culture and geographical area to another cultural group in the same or a distant geographical area for the purpose of sharing the gospel and discipling believers.

Some missiologists have come up with an interesting method for deliniating the various aspects of missions as they relate to cultural and cross-cultural ties, and for a more detailed study of this I would refer you to Ralph D. Winter's writings in chapter nine of a William Carey Library publication entitled *Crucial Dimensions in World Evangelization,* edited by Arthur F. Glasser et al. The definition I am using here would correspond to E-3 missions in Winter's writings.

9

When it comes to a definition of *major* or *majoring*, Webster says:

1. greater in size, amount, number, or extent,
2. constituting the majority,
3. in education—specialization in a field of study; to pursue a principal subject; to specialize in.

Thus, when some organization, be it a church, a school, an association of churches, or even a denomination, claims to be majoring in missions, I assume that the organization means that

> the greater part of its efforts, personnel, finances, and time is directed toward getting the gospel out from that particular area and culture to another culture in the same or a different geographical area.

Over the past twenty-five years my heart and mind have been exercised in many areas. Some impressions have come and gone, others have come and grown stronger with the passing of the years. One such impression, which has become a conviction, is the basis for this book. As stated earlier, it is not an easy conviction to write about, for I realize that it will not be an easy one for some to accept.

That conviction is that *we American evangelicals are kidding ourselves about missions.* I realize that there are those exceptional individuals and local churches who do not fall heir to this criticism, but they are few and far between. Of this I am confident: they will be the author's strongest supporters as he shares his burden.

Beloved, let's quit kidding ourselves about missions.

1

Let's Quit Kidding Ourselves About The Outlook

During a recent furlough in the States, we were living in Fort Collins, Colorado, about seventy miles from downtown Denver, and our deputation schedule called for numerous trips between those two cities. Interstate 25 took us right by Mile High Stadium, where the Denver Broncos professional football team frequently plays. Although I never had opportunity to visit the stadium during a game, I noticed that on some occasions the parking lot was packed to capacity, but at other times the lot would be only partially filled. After some months of observing this, I discovered that there was a relationship between the success ratio of the home-town team and the attendance at the game. Given a string of victories, the team never lacked for a capacity crowd, but let it show a losing streak and there would always be some empty spots in the parking lot. People enjoy backing a winning team.

Francis Rue Steele, in his article "Indifference—Involvement" in the fall 1975 issue of *The Cross and the Cresent* (p. 8) tells us that there are three major sources of error in relation to missions: 1. Ignorance—which produces indifference. 2. Confusion—which produces complacency. 3. Deception—which produces distractions. It is my opinion that Satan is using ignorance on the part of multitudes of evangelical believers in America today to produce indifference. He is using their ignorance of the state of the church worldwide to make them indifferent to the program of world missions. In other words, the mission's parking lot is far from being filled to capacity because God's people are under the impression that the church is losing the game. There are some valid reasons for this negative outlook.

In any warfare it is always important not to let the enemy know if he is being successful, and nowhere is this more evident than in the warfare between heaven and earth. Satan fully realizes the importance of keeping God's people ignorant, and he leaves no stone unturned in his efforts along this line. One effective tool he has today is the news media in the United States, which are controlled by the liberal establishment. One only has to travel outside the United States for a short period of time to realize that Americans are constantly subjected to limited news or one-sided news. Freedom of the press in America means that the liberal element is free to publish just as much of the news as it feels will be beneficial to its cause. This, of course, is especially true in relation to political affairs, but it also has serious implications for the church. For example, American newspapers carried the notice of President Chiang Kai-shek's death in April 1975. But how many of you read in your newspapers about the strong and positive witness for Jesus Christ which the former president of Taiwan had included in his funeral service? In spite of the fact that this world statesman's funeral drew two thousand government officials and special guests and envoys from twenty countries

around the world, and in spite of the fact that Senator
Barry Coldwater had the funeral message included in the
Congressional Record, our liberal press did not consider
it newsworthy to tell us that the funeral message was a
forty-minute address from Hebrews 12: 1-2, which clearly
set forth President Chiang Kai-shek's personal faith and
trust in Jesus Christ. For, after all, what was the liberal
cause to gain by telling the world that this world leader
was a born-again Christian who felt that his fight against
world Communism was related to his faith in Jesus
Christ? Senator Goldwater may not have realized how
significant his question was when he was quoted as saying, "Where else in the world could this happen? I wish
the world could see what I have seen this morning." He
possibly realized that a positive witness like President
Chiang Kai-shek's in a state funeral here in America
would not only be ignored by the home press, it would
result in some demands for equal time by every heretical
and left-wing group around!

Or, turning to another side of the world, we all remember a few years ago when the news media reported
the ouster of all missionaries from Zaire, telling the world
in effect that the church had been thrown out. In a sense it
could be considered a loss for the cause of Christ, so it
was worth reporting. A number of weeks later most of the
ousted missionaries were back in Zaire and they have
been there ever since. But we do not recall seeing that
news in the hometown paper. We did read the report
when the Zairian government confiscated all schools and
took over the public education system the missionaries
had set up in that land. But for some strange reason there
doesn't seem to be any newsworthiness in the fact that
the same government has now called upon the missionary community there to take over once again the task of

public education, a task the government could not handle as effectively as the missions.

A friend who a few years ago was in high places in our government subscribes to a daily newspaper from outside the United States. When asked why, he replied, "In order to get unbiased and objective news, it is necessary." Granted, this is one man's opinion, but it is especially interesting because it comes from one who certainly had some inside information on which to form such an opinion. He, of course, was speaking from the political standpoint, but in the same way that political forces find it to their advantage to censor the news, so does the enemy of our souls. Yes, ignorance produces indifference, and indifference on the part of the church of Jesus Christ makes it much easier for the enemy to accomplish his purpose.

I could cite numerous other illustrations to show how the enemy uses a liberal news media to slant the news and thus contribute to a negative outlook on the part of the church. But there are other methods used as well.

One's focus can also affect his outlook. If, for example, one focuses on the church in Europe today, and on that alone, he is bound to be discouraged, for it is a matter of record that the church in Europe is losing ground. But for that matter the church in America is doing little more than holding its own. Many of the major denominations are recalling their missionary forces from the foreign field and curtailing their ministries locally. It is still common to see some church buildings filled on Sunday morning. Habits don't die easily. But one does not need a stethoscope to realize that there is little life in many of those churches. Even among the more conservative churches in our land today, I believe it is safe to say that one will find by far the larger portion of some congregations seated before the T.V. sets in their living rooms on any given Sunday evening and on Wednesday evening. Well, we blush at even trying to guess the ratio.

Dr. Harold Lindsell's epic book *The Battle for the Bible* certainly pinpoints the crumbling foundations as far as the church in America is concerned. Even the daily newspapers, with their multitude of reports of homosexuality and lesbianism being sanctioned by church groups and permitted not only among the laity but even in the clergy, give ample evidence that America's cup is fast filling up. As far as the Old Testament is concerned, Sodom was guilty of far less wickedness in that the people of that city made no claim of ever knowing God. Certainly Sodomites never had the light and the blessings America has had, and the Scriptures say,

> For unto whomsoever much is given, of him shall be much required [Luke 12:48].

And much of the moral decay evident across the length and breadth of America today is in large measure a result of the breakdown and failure of the institutional church in this land. Even *Time* magazine recognizes this. In an article on pornography in its April 5, 1976, issue *Time* editors write:

> By any definition, porn has mushroomed in the past decade, from a marginal underground cottage industry into an open, aggressive $2 billion-a-year, crime-ridden growth enterprise. Its once powerful foes—*the churches and their antivice allies—are now in retreat if not totally routed* [p. 58, italics added].

No, the outlook certainly isn't very good when we look at Europe or America today. There is little reason for optimism when we have our noses in the newspaper. But, returning to the football stadium, we might draw a comparison with the fan who succumbs to a gloomy depression because as the game goes on he concentrates on the players on the bench and decides all hope is gone because no progress is being made there. He is unaware of the real action.

Satan has succeeded in fooling many Christians about the worldwide program of Jesus Christ, and thus it is that the laborers are so few. In visiting a church recently, I was in a meeting where the people were discussing the results of a recent citywide evangelistic effort sponsored by Campus Crusade for Christ. The folk in that church had made many phone calls and taken part in various other ways. Several weeks after the campaign, they had not one new disciple to show for their efforts and they were concerned about it. One young man, however, being an optimist, wanted to bring in a positive note, so he said, "Well, one real result of all this is the fact that the buttons we wore made it possible for us to discover who else in our offices were believers!" In the same office for three, four, five years and it required a button to get the word out? Somehow I get the impression that some team members are not excited. Could it be that they lack excitement because they are unaware of the action? I am quite confident that this is so. Many evangelical believers in America lack excitement because they lack an awareness of what is happening around the world, and they have a sort of hangdog attitude when it comes to this matter of the outlook for missions. So it is that they respond with, "Leave it to the ladies." And more and more we are hearing, "Leave it to the older ladies," for even the younger ladies are turned off.

Well, for those who might be interested enough to read a bit further, I have some additional information for you which just might have something to do with changing your outlook. If you have found the church in general and missions in particular to be rather boring, may I suggest that you change your focus from the bench to the playing field, for that is where the action is.

If you have been focused on the church in America you have had a narrow field of focus. Notice this diagram, which depicts the world's population:

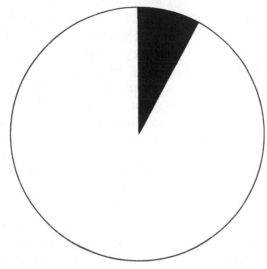

The black portion represents the population of North America (6 percent). For those who have never traveled outside the United States and Canada or have done little or no reading about the rest of the world, it is easy to place far more importance on this portion of the world and the few of us who live here. To the average American, America sets the standard. But what a blow to the young American missionary as he makes his first journey abroad and discovers that fewer people in the world use knives, forks, and spoons than use chopsticks. Furthermore, that same missionary learned long ago that the proper way to drive was on the right side of the road. Proper, that is, until one leaves the 6 percent and goes to Asia. He is amazed to find that well-educated Japanese carpenters cannot work with his American tools because the tools are "backwards." The teeth in Japanese saws are set so the instrument cuts when being pulled toward the one using it, and the same is true of the Japanese plane. And the list of differences could fill many books.

The missionary soon learns, at least he had better soon learn if he hopes to meet with any success, that his background has given him a very limited knowledge of the world and the people living in it. As an American, he possibly understands 6 percent of the world's people (and that is possibly an exaggeration, since the 6 percent includes various minority groups in the United States). But what about the other 94 percent? So it is with those whose outlook is based on their knowledge of the American church. They only have 6 percent of the picture.

To gain a proper outlook of the church we must first of all consider what the Word of God has to say about it. Two thousand years ago Jesus said, "I will build my church; and the gates of hell shall not prevail against it"(Matt. 16:18), but the average believer today is not too much different from the followers of Jesus in His day. Jesus had told them time and time again of His coming death, burial, and resurrection. He warned them not to be surprised and He sought to prepare them for those events. However, the believers had not really paid attention to what He said, and when those fateful days took place, every one of Christ's disciples fled in fear and disillusionment. Those women who loved Him so much took the spices and ointment and went out to the tomb fully expecting to find His body there—which, by the way, points out the real possibility of our possessing a deep love for the Savior and of our being very sincere in our service for Him while at the same time we are acting in disobedience because we missed what He told us. I am convinced that much today that is being done in the church and on the mission field—much of which is being done as a result of a heart full of love for Jesus Christ—is not going to be acceptable to Him simply because it is not in accord with what He has said. Sincerity means nothing when it ignores the written Word of God. We will deal more specifically with this later.

Jesus' followers did not find His body there on that resurrection morning. Notice the rebuke that was given in Luke 24: 6-8:

> He is not here, but is risen: *remember how he spoke* unto you when he was yet in Galilee, saying, The Son of man must be delivered into the hands of sinful men, and be crucified, and the third day rise again. *And they remembered his words* [italics added].

Or, again, in Matthew 28:6, where the angel said:

> He is not here: for he is risen, *as he said* [italics added].

Before we come down too hard on those early followers, however, let's think about something else He said. Something we have had in print for our study and consideration. Something we have heard many sermons about; yes, something many of us have committed to memory, and still it doesn't seem to sink in. Think carefully of it now.

> *I* will build my church; and the gates of hell shall not prevail against it [Matt. 16:18, italics added].

Notice that carefully. Who is going to build the church?

Not you and I, not the mission board or the missionary. Not the bright Greek and Hebrew scholar who just graduated from seminary. Not the powerful preacher with a fleet of ninety-five Sunday school buses. Not the preacher with a plan for explosion. "I, Jesus Christ, am going to build My church."

Turn to Exodus 3 and notice a beautiful illustration of what I am trying to say here. God has called Moses aside for a very special message following a forty-year preparatory course he just completed in God's Desert University. God says, "And *I* am come down to deliver them [the children of Israel] out of the hand of the Egyptians" (v.8, italics added). Have you noticed carefully what God said? Moses missed the point at first and almost blew it. As a matter of fact, it was only the mercy of God that kept Moses from losing out altogether. Now notice verse 10, where God further develops His plan and program: "Come now therefore, and I will send thee unto Pharaoh, that thou mayest bring forth my people the children of Israel out of Egypt." Now listen to Moses. "Who am I, that I should go unto Pharaoh?" (v.11). God replies in verse 12, "I will be with thee." God said very plainly, "*I* am come down to deliver them." At that point in history the children of Israel were as good as delivered. God said that He was going to do it, and Moses should have had enough sense to realize that the matter was settled then and there.

Jesus Christ told His disciples that He was going to the cross, that He would go to the tomb, and that on resurrection morning He would rise again. Those disciples should have had a prayer and praise service at the cross and the first Easter sunrise service to welcome the Lord out of the tomb. But what actually happened? They fled in terror, disorganized, discouraged, and dismayed. All of this simply because they failed to listen to what their Lord said.

Today many of Christ's followers are basically in the same condition, and for the same reason. They have failed to pay attention to what Jesus Christ has said. Jesus said, "I will build my church," and that is exactly what He is doing around the world today.

When the children of Israel were at the edge of the Red Sea and they saw the chariots of Pharaoh racing down upon them, they had reason to become fearful if they had missed what God had said to Moses, "I am come down to deliver them." But if they had really paid attention to His word, they could have enjoyed the events God had planned for them.

Likewise, if we today know and believe what God has told us in His Word it will result in some drastic changes on our part. Actually, we are involved in a contest, the outcome of which has already been announced.

> Wherefore God also hath highly exalted him, and given him a name which is above every name: that at the name of Jesus every knee should bow, of things in heaven, and things in earth, and things under the earth; and that every tongue should confess that Jesus Christ is Lord, to the glory of God the Father [Phil. 2:9-11].

Every knee shall bow, every tongue shall confess. It's all settled! It is *all* settled. It is as sure as the drowning of the Egyptian army and the empty cross or the empty tomb. It is as certain as the risen Christ. Why then the cry for the leeks, the onions, and the garlic of Egypt? Why the horrible denials of our modern day Peters, the empty pews on Sunday night, and powerless midweek prayer services? Why is it that after two thousand years the laborers are still few? There can only be one reason. Like the children of Israel and Moses, like the early disciples, God's people today simply are not listening to what He has said, or even worse, they do not believe Him.

The dark picture of the church in Europe and the discouraging overall picture of the church in North America notwithstanding, the worldwide picture of the church is fantastic, because Jesus said, "I will build," and that is exactly what He is doing. When you hear the missionary crying about the closed or closing doors, you can check him off as another believer who has not paid attention to the words of the Lord Jesus Christ. When you hear the frantic appeals tied to such things as the lateness of the hour, the apparent failure due to scarcity of finances and personnel, or even the onslaught of godless Communism, mark it down in your little book that those making such appeals have not heard the Lord Jesus Christ correctly.

Some may say, "Is it not true that there are closed doors to the gospel today?" There certainly are. Some are closed and others may be closing. But allow me to demonstrate something. Turn to the next page right now. Take a piece of paper and as briefly as possible describe what you see on that page. Now, did you mention the vast white area on the page in your description, or did you focus simply on the little mark that occupies one minute area? Why do we generally tend to magnify the insignificant? Ninety-nine percent of the page was clean and white, but did you really notice that? As you look at the world today and point out the countries with the closed doors, please allow me to point out those with open doors. My list will be considerably longer than yours.

Again, if you are really concerned about closed doors perhaps you should consider the message of Revelation 3:7 where we read:

> These things saith he that is holy, he that is true, he that
> hath the key of David, *he that openeth, and no man shut-*
> *teth; and shutteth, and no man openeth* [italics added].

Did you get that? Who shuts doors? Who opens doors?
You see, when we pay attention to what our Lord has said,
when we get the facts from the Word, and when we believe those facts, we automatically have a vastly different
outlook. For then we can face the closed doors of a Red
Sea and be at complete peace even though the enemy's
forces are in sight. "I will build my church." "I open and
no man closes." "I close and no man opens." Consider, for
example, how our Lord is able, believe it or not, to use
closed doors for His own glory. A number of years ago
God allowed Satan to tap a man by the name of Mao on
the shoulder and suggest to him that he send some of his
"peace corps" to east Africa. Mao thought it a good idea
and sent thousands. Missionaries and other Christians in
those east Africa nations, however, had not got the message that doors were closed, and they availed themselves
of the opportunity to share Christ with some of those Red
Chinese soldiers. There are reports of over two hundred of
those soldiers who have received Jesus Christ as Savior
and have since been flown back behind those "closed
doors" of China. You will understand when I point out
that closed doors work from both sides. Those on the
outside cannot get in, but those on the inside cannot get
out. Now what do you suppose those Chinese Christians
are doing? We have no way of knowing at this time, but no
doubt some have already paid with their blood for their
testimony. Defeat again? Not when we realize that the
blood of the martyrs has always been the seed of the
church. And Jesus Christ is building His church, even in
Red China.

For many, many years the land of Tibet has been off limits to the Christian message. What is the Lord doing about that? He simply allowed the Red Chinese forces to invade that land, forcing the Dalai Lama, the religious leader of the Tibetan people, to flee for his life. During the dramatic escape, the Lord of the harvest brought the Dalai Lama into close contact with people who in a normal situation would never be allowed to see or speak with their ruler. Some of those who gave the fleeing Dalai Lama refuge were able to tell him about the King of kings and to place the Word of God in his hands. We know today that the seed has been sown. Without the closed doors and the Communist invasion, that would not have been possible. Closed doors? So what? They may pose problems to us, but only when we have failed to pay attention to God's Word.

Do you know that the church today is growing faster than at any time since Pentecost? Did you know that Christ's church exists in every country of the world with only two possible exceptions? Muslim Mauritania in Africa and Mongolia in Asia are the only two nations on earth where we do not know of any organized body of believers meeting in public or secretly. At this time we do know that the gospel is going into even those lands. I understand that there are two Mongolian Christians on the staff of an Evangelical Alliance Mission radio station in Korea. Every day they are beaming the gospel message over the mountains into their native land, so it is even possible today that the Lord has a branch of His church already established there.

Are you aware of the fact that between fifty and seventy thousand souls a day are being added to Christ's church around the world? In east Africa alone twenty thousand per day are receiving Jesus Christ as Lord and Savior.

Mission leaders tell us that if the present growth rate continues until the end of this century, Africa will be over 50 percent professing Christian. They also tell us that for the first time in history Christians outnumber Muslims and animists in Africa south of the Sahara. Are you starting to feel a bit of excitement? Well, stay with me, because there is more to follow.

What do you know about the Bible and the languages of the world? Into how many languages and dialects has God's Word been translated? The Koran, the Muslim holy book, is in about a hundred languages, while the Word of God is in over sixteen hundred! Ninety percent of the world's population have the Word of God available to them in their own language, if they can read. Another 5 percent have the New Testament available, and another 3 percent have at least one book of the Bible. That adds up to the thrilling fact that 98 percent of the people on the earth, if they can read, have at least a portion of the Word of God ready for them. And Wycliffe Bible Translators have set 1985 as their goal for getting the Bible into every language. They are presently working in over 660 tribes in twenty-five countries, and the goal is in sight within our generation.

Have you been kidding yourself about the outlook for world missions? If so, may I encourage you to pull your head out of the sand long enough to take a good look around? And start that look with the Book. Are these things I have been writing about surprising to you? The disciples were surprised by Christ's resurrection, too, so you are in good company.

Well, it would be impossible even to begin to tell it all here, but let's go just a bit further. Something new has been taking place in our day, and it concerns third world missions, missions in the developing nations. Third world churches are very much alive and growing, even to the point of sending out national missionaries to other nations. Dr. Virgil Gerber tells of his visit to one church in Korea where he discovered that it had a membership of over thirty thousand people. In speaking with the pastor, he learned that the membership was divided into 1,311 neighborhood groups, each with a leader. Those leaders meet in the main church building every Tuesday morning, where they are instructed for two hours via closed-circuit color television. There are fifty-five full-time pastors and five Sunday worship services, since the auditorium only seats ten thousand. And we here in America speak of Korea as a mission field! Yes, we are aware of some very real problems in Christ's church in Korea. There is a very real need for the larger churches there to gain a vision and burden for the multitudes of smaller, struggling groups in the rural areas. As in the United States, even so in Korea, many pastors are concerned only with their own work, their own people, their own projects. But God is at work. Everything is on schedule, and I count it a privilege to be involved in what Jesus Christ is doing around the world in our day.

Another thrilling facet of world missions today is the area of technology. Dr. J. Herbert Kane, author, educator, and authority on world missions, wrote in the March 1977 issue of *Emissary:*

> Modern technology has made it possible to proclaim the Good News to all the world. Today there are sixty-five radio stations owned and operated by Christian missions in the Third World. Most of these are small with local coverage. Others are large and powerful enough to beam the gospel around the world by short wave. One of these stations in Manila is broadcasting the gospel daily from 25 transmitters in 73 languages to more than two billion

people in Asia. Every month 18,000 letters are received from almost 60 countries. More than 1,500,000 have enrolled in Bible correspondence courses. The operation requires a full-time staff of 400 [p. 4].

Dr. Kane sums it up in this way:

For the first time in history we have the tools and the techniques to finish the job of world evangelization in one generation. The only problem is *manpower*. Can we get the right kind of missionary in sufficient numbers to complete the task? [p. 5].

I respond to Dr. Kane's question thus: Jesus Christ said two thousand years ago that He would build His church, so we can be assured that He will secure the necessary workers and the necessary finances to complete the task. The real question is:

Are we going to get involved? Is the American church going to rise to the challenge while the opportunity to do so remains, or must Jesus Christ raise up another national church in another country to complete His building program?

Any student of history will recall that hundreds of years ago God used the nation of Spain to send out Christian missionaries into the then-known world. The time came when Spain and its church turned from God, and God turned to Germany to carry on His purposes. Then Germany turned to rationalism and God turned to the British Empire to send out His messengers around the world. Alas, the time came when Britain, too, turned its back upon God, and America fell heir to the missionary mantle. But God forbid that our American egotism should blind us to reality. God forbid that Satan should cause us to believe that God's last opportunity rests with us. It well may be that Jesus Christ is right now preparing His church in Japan, or in Korea, or in some other land, to carry on the task of getting the gospel out to the rest of the world. He is by no means limited to the United States and Canada.

Have you been kidding yourself about the outlook for missions? Are you one of those many believers in America who have not been involved because they are not really aware that there is much in which to be involved? Jesus Christ is still offering high-paying shares of stock to those of His church in this country, and elsewhere, who are interested enough to pay the price of involvement.

Let's quit kidding ourselves about the outlook for world missions.

2

Let's Quit Kidding Ourselves About the Reason

One has only to turn the pages of any Christian periodical that carries paid advertisements to discover the great confusion within the church today concerning the reason for missions. Almost any issue of those magazines confronts the public with an array of crying babies, orphans, and scenes of famine, war, or pestilence done up in a sort of Christian Madison Avenue promotional appeal for your missionary dollar.

If our reason for giving, or if our reason for personal involvement, is based on any such appeal, we are kidding ourselves about the reason for missions.

Certainly the Word of God teaches a responsibility toward orphans and widows in the church, but feeding orphans and widows is not missions. Nor is it the reason for missions. It may strike you as a cold and brutal point, but nowhere in the Scriptures are we commanded to go into all the world and feed the orphans. However, a program is set forth which, if followed, will result in groups of people being saved and discipled and formed into local churches, and then those local churches will be able to minister more effectively to the spiritual and social needs of the people around them.

The reason for missions is not related to the fact that we have so much and they so little. The reason for missions is not welfare or economics or education or medicine. If all men were rich, the need for missions would still be the same. If all men were educated, if all were well fed, if all had good jobs, the great commission would continue to maintain its importance and its urgency.

Needless to say, there is great need for caution when dealing with a subject like this, for we are dealing with far more than just finances. Many wonderful, dedicated, evangelical believers are involved in ministries around the world which they sincerely believe are in the context of "biblical missions," and they will react strongly to anything I might say which would question the validity of their thinking. This reaction I must expect. What I am more concerned about is the possibility of reaction that may arise from a misunderstanding of what I am seeking to point up, so I emphasize here that I have no intention of judging any ministry or activity per se. Of every believer it can be said, "To his own master he stands or falls." What I am saying is that the Word of God gives us one definite reason for missions, and unless our basis for missions falls in line with the Word, we are kidding ourselves about the reason for missions.

Furthermore, it is my conviction that a failure to understand the biblical reason for missions may well result in a lot of sincere activity that someday will be revealed as worthless—the wood, hay, and stubble of 1 Corinthians 3.

It would seem that many of God's people, and some who are not His, base their missionary activity on emotion, for they become involved only when emotionally stirred. This category must include a great number of people, judging by the high-priced ads in Christian periodicals. Crying babies, emaciated bodies, scenes of famine or war. Thus it is that the missionary who is an effective speaker and can paint word pictures of the suffering and anguish of those with whom he works can secure vast amounts of financial support. He works on the emotions.

Then there are those mission speakers who can hit pay dirt by working on the guilt complex so many have today. "You have so much and they have so little." Needless to say, all kinds of angles can be worked here. Certainly some speakers are more tactful than others in this approach, but the reasoning is the same. Here we find the "give up a meal for those who are starving" mentality. The possibility that giving up a meal might just be of great physical benefit to ourselves personally does not even enter our minds. No, we have soothed our guilty conscience a bit, we have exhibited some wonderful spirit of sacrifice. After all, we have so much, and what is one little meal? Besides, there is a big roast in the oven for the next meal.

Next is that group of people who have a measure of involvement in missions because of, believe it or not, their sin nature. They have a strong desire to do something to gain God's approval. They faced this at the time of their salvation and it continues on throughout their Christian experience. Of course, biblical Christianity has no monoply on this type of person. If the facts were known, we would probably find a large percentage of those involved in liberal Christian missions under this heading, and some of those people will put many evangelicals to shame when it comes to sincerity, dedication, and involvement. Nevertheless, I believe that they too are kidding themselves about the reason for missions.

The author of the book of Hebrews speaks of those who "through fear of death were all their lifetime subject to bondage" (2:15), and certainly the same can be said in our day concerning many both in and out of the church. Only eternity will reveal how much religious effort man has put forth simply as a result of the inborn sin nature and its natural tendency to try to please God via the means of good works.

Yet another rationale given for missions is simply human reason. This category is best represented by a statement made famous by a well-known missionary statesman: "Why should any man hear the message twice before all have heard it once?" This is somewhat similar to the first category mentioned, "emotional appeal," for it certainly does appeal to our emotions. However, the fallacy of this kind of reasoning should be evident to any thinking person, and evidence certainly seems to indicate that not even the man who popularized this statement really believes it, or else how could he continue preaching to the same congregation for many, many years? Nowhere in Scripture do we find anything that would support such logic, if we can call it logic, and just try to imagine the worldwide results if our missionaries around the world followed such reasoning.

Sad to say, some missionaries in Japan have followed this philosophy to a degree, and as a result they have created havoc for many of their fellow missionaries. While most missionaries will settle in a given location in order to win the friendship of the local people and then start sharing the Word in any one of many different ways, the group to whom I refer will pass through a town or village, blaring out a gospel message via a high-powered amplifier and speakers. The message proclaimed is 100 percent scripturally sound. The audience is told that there is only one God, that they were born in sin and are hell bound, that Jesus is the only way, and that all their gods are false. "Repent and be baptized or go to hell," they are told. When these missionaries drive out of a village, several things have happened to make Satan rejoice. First, the traveling missionaries are convinced that they have "evangelized" the village. Second, their crude method of "fulfilling the Great Commission" has turned the nationals against both those who did the "evangelizing" and against the resident missionary, who has spent weeks, months, or even years living among the people, trying to build some bridges of understanding and friendship in order to prepare the way for a fruitful harvest.And a fruitful harvest requires not only the sowing of the seed; it also requires a discipling of the fruit that comes forth.

Finally, although there are no doubt other nonscriptural or extrascriptural reasons set forth for missions, I must mention one more, for wide is the gate and many there be that find it. I refer to the large numbers of God's people who respond to a missionary program as a result of uninformed enthusiasm.

There are far too many possible illustrations available for this point for me to describe them all since that is not the basic point of this book, but bear with me for just a few.

First of all, there are those who love to give out the Word of God in printed form because they know that God has said He will honor His Word. Here again I urge caution as you read this, for I am in no wise finding fault with the motive involved here. The Word of God is quick and powerful, and the annals of Christian history are filled with the testimonies of those who have come to a saving knowledge of Jesus Christ through simply reading a portion of the Word of God in a hotel room, prison, or hospital ward. What I refer to are those who in some manner hear of a desire for Bibles in some faraway place and, without any means of evaluating the legitimacy of the request or the ability of the receiver to read that Bible, they send beautiful leather-bound copies.

In a few cases, where thank-you notes are received, the donors are assured that they are carrying on a great missionary work. What they never receive is a full report of what was accomplished with those Bibles and why the receivers were so happy to get them. Certainly what I am telling you now is not always what happens to Bibles sent overseas, but in one case known to me, Bibles sent to India were well received simply for the leather bindings. The covers were removed to make purses and wallets, and the books themselves discarded. Yes, the gift Bibles proved to be a real blessing, a financial blessing, to those who received them. But I am quite confident that that was not exactly what the doner had in mind when he responded to an uninformed enthusiasm.

Another way in which uninformed enthusiasm can wreak havoc is when a foreign national circulates among American churches to secure financial backing for his program or ministry. How many of God's people have gone off the deep end at this point! Deeply committed to foreign missions, they open wide their pocketbooks and again Satan is overjoyed."Just think, we are directly supporting a national. He has the language and is doing such a sacrificial work, and 100 percent of what we give is going into the work." But how do you know what the national is doing? How do you know how your gifts are being used? How do you know your direct giving is really good stewardship? You don't. And if you are being motivated into financial involvement in missions through uninformed enthusiasm, do not be surprised to discover at the judgment seat of Christ that your investment has not paid off.

And what has been said about the foreign national can also be said about many missionaries. I am well aware that what I am about to share with you is personal opinion. But it is opinion arrived at after almost thirty years in Christian ministry, and it is opinion that I believe deserves a hearing. It is my definite opinion that churches and individuals in the homeland should think twice, maybe three times, before taking on the support of independent missionaries, *unless* the donors have a very definite and effective means of investigating that work. And a whirlwind tour of the mission fields is not an effective means of investigating! Let's face it, any missionary with an average amount of intelligence can come up with something to show and tell if he has twenty-four hours' notice. Yes, he is a great speaker at home. He may even be a great spiritual blessing in your church. But your uninformed enthusiasm is not a scriptural reason for your missionary involvement.

Some time ago a young college student in one of our meetings asked why a mission board is necessary. There are many valid reasons for the existence of mission boards, but perhaps none is of greater importance than the one of which I write now. A very important responsibility of a mission board is the supervision of its missionaries. Few local churches are equipped to supervise and objectively administer oversight of their overseas outreaches. By working together with other local churches through qualified and trustworthy mission boards, any church can have the assurance that its missionary dollars and its missionary personnel are well placed and well supervised. Missionaries are usually hardworking people, but they can get away with laziness more easily than a pastor in the homeland. And when a missionary gets away with laziness, the missionary is certainly not the only one at fault.

Laziness, however, is not the only cause, nor is it the main cause, for my expressing concern over the independent worker. As a matter of fact, I have heard about lazy missionaries but have never met one. What I have met are a few who are involved in all kinds of activities that the supporters back home know nothing about, and others who are not producing in the very areas for which they were sent to the mission field. Again, there are some who receive full support from the homeland, but nobody knows how much is received or how it is used. I know of one missionary who received money for land and for a building for a local church, but, lo and behold, when that missionary passed away, the property went to his adopted daughter, and then to her adopted daughter when she passed away. That property today is in no way related to the Lord's work. How many tens of thousands of dollars of the Lord's money have gone this route only eternity will reveal. And it is all given as a result of uninformed enthusiasm.

I have also heard, while home in America, about churches a missionary has started on his field, but when I talk to other missionaries from that field they know nothing about those churches. Such letters and claims are rather difficult to publish when there is adequate supervision. Having said all this, however, in all fairness I must go on to say that I know that there are some independent missionaries who are worthy of the support they receive. They are faithful workers, fruitful workers, honest stewards. Nevertheless, I sincerely believe I ask a very legitimate question when I ask, are you supporting missions or a missionary through uninformed enthusiasm? Certainly you have confidence in those to whom you give, but on what is your confidence based? And what I write about foreign missions is equally true when it comes to any other Christian ministry, especially radio and T.V. programs. One thing is certain. Some of the wrongs would be corrected if God's people always insisted on full and complete financial statements that reveal total income and how it is used. Note, however, that I say, "some of the wrongs," for some people do not bother to look over such financial statements if they are provided. When some well-known Christian groups can put out financial statements which show that they use 60 percent of all gifts for administration (mainly high salaries) that 40 percent or less actually gets out to the mission field for the designated purpose, and God's people continue to give, it proves that somebody is not thinking.

I have already referred to the matter of the orphans, but perhaps a further word is in order. A few years ago I was asked in a public meeting about my views on this business of supporting orphans. At that time I shared my twofold concern. First, supporting orphans is not missions. Second, most people who support orphans really have no way of knowing how their gifts are used. I then went on to cite the story of a widow who had done housework to earn money to support an orphan overseas. After several years of sending support, the lady saved enough money to make a visit to the overseas orphanage. She stopped on the way to visit friends in Japan. They told of her excitement as she looked forward to meeting "her orphan." Some of the missionaries in Tokyo expressed concern, however, when they learned that this woman was paying a surprise visit to the orphanage in another country, for they knew what a surprise it was going to be, not for the orphan, but for the widow. Without going into detail, I'll only say that she was a brokenhearted woman when she returned through Tokyo. Any similarity between the magazine ads and the promotional literature she had received and what she actually found upon her arrival was purely accidental. Hers was a case of uninformed enthusiasm. When I finished telling the story, a gentleman in the church where I was speaking stood and said, "I am sure what our brother has just told you is true. We need special caution in this area. But I have been supporting orphans for years now, and I know the organization I give through is honest and aboveboard. My orphan even writes to me."

Following the service the pastor asked me for the name of the organization I had spoken about, and I told him my purpose was not to speak against certain organizations but to promote certain principles and to challenge God's people to think. The pastor then told me the name of the organization the gentleman was supporting, and guess what? It was the same one our widow had been supporting. She had been fooling herself on two matters. She thought she was supporting missions and she thought she was being a good steward. She has, by the way, stopped fooling herself on both counts.

Yes, there are all sorts of reasons set forth for missionary involvement, all sorts of challenges presented in an effort to secure finances and personnel. The need, the untold millions, the crying orphans, our wealth and their poverty, and on and on. But the only sure, undeniable, and inescapable reason for missions is the command of our Commander in Chief. He said, "Go." He said, "Give." He said, "Pray." And we need no other reason. When the church of Jesus Christ falls in love with Jesus Christ, it will become a missionary church.

If ye love me, keep my commandments [John 14:15].
But whoso keepeth his word, in him verily is the love of
God perfected: hereby know we that we are in him [1 John
2:5]

I have written at length of the various nonscriptural and
even unscriptural motives behind missions today, and I
have considered activities that some people call missions
but that I do not believe are in any way related to the Great
Commission. However, to point out error is one thing. To
come up with ways and means of correcting error is
something else. It is my desire to suggest in this book
such ways and means, so we must go to the Word of God.
Since the whole business of missions starts with God's
Word, it is only logical that we use it as our standard and
guide.

Thus it is that I can make the statement that the command of the Lord Jesus Christ, our Commander in Chief, is
the only 100 percent sure, undeniable, and inescapable
reason for missions. But why is it so important to determine *the* biblical reason for missions? Why do I think it
necessary to call attention to some who, in my thinking at
least, are either involved in mission activity as a result of
a nonscriptural or unscriptural motive or who are wrong
in even thinking they are involved in missions at all?

It is simply because, as I pointed out in chapter one, the
basic problem in missions today is the same problem
Jesus pointed out to His followers two thousand years
ago. The harvest is great but the laborers are few. Too few
of God's people are involved in the primary task He gave
to the church. In chapter one I suggested that part of the
reason for the scarcity of laborers is the tragic fact that too
many born-again people are totally unaware of what is
happening in the church worldwide in this day and age.
If they were aware of the facts, they would be excited and

would want to be involved. In this chapter we are dealing with reason number two, the scarcity of laborers—for Satan has many confused about the real reason for missions and, as was pointed out in the previous chapter, ignorance (in relation to missions) produces indifference and confusion produces complacency.

That many today are confused in the area of missions should be evident to any thinking person who looks over the so-called mission program in the average American church. Most of us are certainly pro-missions, so we want the missions budget to look as good as possible, and to accomplish this we include everything possible under that heading. I once knew of a pastor who considered his Sunday school program as missions. Certainly the Sunday school can and should be a vital and fruitful part of any local church ministry, but it is easy to see how one might become complacent about *real* missions if he were to think of such a Sunday school program as missions. And the same could be said about church day schools or Bible schools or seminaries supported by the local church.

But of utmost concern to me today is the tremendous lack of interest in missions on the part of the great host of young people in our churches. Urbana 1976 produced some thrilling results, with thousands of young people signing decision cards indicating their intention to move out into the fields white unto harvest. However, one very important matter should be of great concern to all of us who love the local church, and to local church pastors especially. The vast majority of those who made such decisions were young men and women less than five years old in the Lord. In other words, they were not basically young people raised in our churches. Where are the youth who have been brought up in our churches? Where are the young people from our Christian homes? It is my conviction that many of them have been turned off as far as missions are concerned, and one of the turning off factors has been the unscriptural and nonscriptural logic behind our missionary efforts. While certain traditional ways still seem to produce results for some of us, the young people of today can see through much of the hypocrisy, sham, or pure emotionalism we have operated under, and they simply are not interested. If, however, we can return to the Word of God and give those young people some statements beginning "thus saith the Lord," something will happen. And it will happen among the older folk as well, although to break with tradition is difficult.

A number of books in the bookstores deal with the problem being faced in world missions in our day. Many of those books have much food for thought, and anyone involved in missions, whether it is the missionary himself or a member of a local church missionary committee, would do well to keep abreast of what is being written in this field. Nevertheless, I wonder if there is not a tendency to focus too much on the problems of missions and not enough on the One who commands missions. We hear, for example, that we have a different breed of young people today and that they are not so quick to respond to career service, that short-term service programs appeal to them more. J. Herbert Kane states it well in the revised edition of his book *Winds of Change in the Christian Mission* (Chicago: Moody, 1976):

> This is one reason for the popularity of the short-term program. It affords an opportunity to engage in mission-ary work *without making a long-term commitment* [pp. 22-23, italics added].

The disturbing thing is that too many of us seem ready and willing to accept this present situation as a fact of life about which nothing can be done. But this problem is nothing new. The church has faced it in every age. Jesus Himself faced it in His day. When the rich young ruler asked for some short-term assignment—"What must I do?"—Jesus asked for a long-term commitment and we hear no more of that young man.

Quoting again from J. Herbert Kane:

> This sense of urgency is missing from modern missionary literature [p. 45].

And I add that it is also missing from too many pulpits in our land today.

Some time ago, while attending a summer camp for high schoolers, I was distressed to find that missions hardly had a spot on the week's program. That camp for many years had spotlighted missions, and many missionaries had made their commitment for service there and are presently serving around the world. When I spoke to the camp leaders of my concern, they replied, "But, Jim, our young people today are not interested in missions!" If that is so, and it seems to be, why is it so?

I believe there are two basic reasons. In the first place, the various unscriptural reasons for missions which we have just considered, the reasons that motivate so much of our missionary activity today, simply leave young people cold. They see through the shallowness and hypocrisy of it all and, frankly, they couldn't care less. Human logic, which may have moved man to action in one generation, will often fall on deaf ears in the next generation.

The second reason I cite for the lack of interest in missions on the part of young people is the plain and simple fact that we have had a breakdown in three areas: the Bible schools and seminaries, the pulpit, and the Christian home. It is rather difficult to pinpoint where the breakdown started, for all three institutions feed upon one another. But I am inclined to believe that the solution to our problem will never be realized permanently unless something happens in the schools, which will affect the pulpits, which will in turn affect out families.

Dr. Harold Lindsell, in *The Battle for the Bible* (Grand Rapids: Zondervan, 1976), ably points out:

> As the seminaries go, so go the churches. Almost inevitably, graduates of a theological institution reflect the viewpoints of their teachers [p. 197].

In other words, if there is fire in the Bible school and in the seminary, there will be fire in the pulpit. And if there is fire in the pulpit, there will be fire in the pew.

Perhaps I can best illustrate what I am trying to say by telling you about a discussion I recently had with a leader in a particular evangelical movement. This man is active in trying to help churches secure pastors and in helping seminary graduates find churches. During the course of our conversation, he made the statement that less than one-third of the seminary graduates he met were qualified to serve as pastors and that a very large percentage of them were basically interested in two things: First, how much salary can I expect? Second, how much time off can I expect?

Is it possible that our pulpits and theological schools have unintentionally contributed to that type of mentality by a gradual departure from the message of commitment which came from the lips of our Lord Himself? I think it is possible. But I will deal with this more fully in another chapter.

While I am pressing for an acknowledgment that the sole biblical reason for missions is the Lord's command, I certainly do acknowledge that the Scriptures make it abundantly clear why He has commanded us to go, and a good knowledge of the reasons behind the command will certainly add urgency to our response. However, I continue to insist that our obedience, in order to be pleasing to our Lord, must be based on His command and not on our understanding of the reasons behind His command.

What are the basic reasons behind the command?

1. All men are sinners and separated from God (Isa. 59:2; John 3:36; Rom. 3:23).
2. Man apart from Jesus Christ is eternally lost (John 3:36; 1 John 2:2).
3. Jesus is not willing that any should perish (2 Pet. 3:9).
4. Man has no means of knowing God's plan of redemption through Jesus Christ aside from the Word of God (Rom. 10:9-17).

A close examination of missionary work around the world today will reveal much evidence to support the contention that many of God's people in days past have fooled themselves about the reason for missions. Intentions may have been the best, sincerity the watchword, and love the motive, but nevertheless there are piles of wood, hay, and stubble in the forms of giant schools, orphanages, hospitals, and church buildings where Jesus Christ is very much a stranger today. Much of this is due to the fact that human logic received priority over the Word of God.

3

Let's Quit Kidding Ourselves About The Call

Over the past nineteen hundred years, the church has been confronted with a great array of problems, and legion are the volumes that have been written about those problems. However, one problem that faced the church before its actual inception and has continued to face the church down through the centuries it that which Jesus spoke about to His disciples when He said, "The harvest truly is plenteous, but the labourers are few" (Matt. 9:37). When Jesus spoke those words He and His disciples were looking out on a world with a population slightly less than the population of the United States today. Historians tell us that in Jesus' day the world population was between two hundred and two hundred fifteen million. If the harvest was great then, how can we find an adequate word to describe what it is now? And if the laborers were few then, comparatively speaking, they are far fewer today. The question that continually rings in my heart and in my mind, the question that is the basis for this book, is: Why are the laborers still few?

In the first chapter, I suggested that one reason for the scarcity of laborers is that many of God's people are kidding themselves about the outlook for the church. They do not realize what is taking place today around the world under the banner of the cross; they have not comprehended the importance of Christ's statement, "I will build my church" (Matt. 16:18); and they are not aware of the fact that the Captain of our faith has everything under His control, everything in the universe.

In chapter two I dealt with another reason for the scarcity of laborers when I pointed out the various ideas people have concerning the reason for missions. Francis Steele has said that confusion produces complacency, and there is certainly a great deal of confusion concerning the reason for missions; thus we have complacency and a shortage of workers.

I would now like to consider another very important reason for the scarcity of laborers—namely, the great confusion that centers on what we refer to as "the call." How many books have been written about the missionary and his call I do not know, but I am convinced that there is a great and desperate need to get back to the Book for a fresh look at the subject in order that we might quit kidding ourselves about the call.

When I am speaking to a group, it is not unusual for someone to say, "Tell us about your call to Japan," and I generally receive a surprised reaction when I respond, "I was never called to Japan." Now I understand what the people mean by their question, but my contention at this point is that they are not actually saying what they mean. Allow me to illustrate.

Missionaries in Japan have always been confronted with numbers of Japanese wanting to learn or practice English conversation. All school children from seventh grade up are required to study English, and many of them become quite good in English grammar. Conversation,

however, is very difficult for many Japanese because of
the limited number of English teachers who can speak
English as a native tongue. Most Japanese English
teachers speak English with a strong Japanese accent;
thus their students speak a sort of Japanese English. Especially is this true in rural areas. When a foreigner
comes to town he is often confronted with many, many
opportunities to assist both students and professional
people with conversational English. Now, put yourself in
the shoes of one of those Japanese who has studied English. You have a reasonably good vocabulary and you
enjoy talking to the American missionary as a means of
improving your pronunication. During the course of a
conversation one day, the missionary looks at his watch
and exclaims, "Oh, you will have to excuse me, I have to
catch a train for Tokyo."

"You have to what?"

"I have to catch a train for Tokyo."

"Catch a train? Isn't that dangerous? Wouldn't it be
safer for you to wait until it stops and then get in?"

You see, we speak about *catching* a plane or train (or
taking a plane to such and such a place, or riding *on* a
train), when what we really mean is that we are going to
meet and board a plane or train, which will then take us to
our destination. Now, those of us who speak English as
our native tongue have no problem using such expres-
sions, because we understand each other's usage,
Nevertheless, we are not really saying what we mean—or
we do not really mean what we are saying.

The same thing is usually true when people speak of a
missionary call, for most of the time they do not mean
call at all—they mean *direction*. I am convinced that a
large segment of the church today is guilty of fuzzy thinking about what the call of God is. I have already men-

tioned the need for a return to the Word of God in order to gain a proper perspective of the entire subject of missions, and nowhere is this more needful than when we are considering the matter of the call of God. When you think of this subject, what scriptural passages spring into your mind?

Isaiah 6:8, where we find the words, "Whom shall I send, and who will go for us?"

The book of Jonah, where we find the command, "Go to Nineveh" (1:2).

Acts 16:9, where we read of Paul's hearing the cry, "Come over into Macedonia, and help us."

There is a good reason for those verses to pop into your mind when you hear the word *call* for you have been programed that way. All your Christian life you have heard lots of missionary speakers quoting these passages and, no doubt, Matthew 28: 19-20 is the most popular and best known of all such passages. But will it surprise you if I say that not one of these passages has anything to do with a call? Will it upset you for me to say that Jesus was not calling anybody when He spoke the words of Matthew 28: 19-20? Well, I really do not want to upset you, but the fact of the matter is there is no call there. The call had come much earlier, and Jesus is simply giving directions to His followers at this point. Check your favorite Greek scholar (I did mine), and you will find that Jesus never said, "Go ye therefore" (Matt. 28:19). He said, "Going, . . . teach all nations." Jesus was not telling His followers to go out into all the world; He was telling them what to do when they did in fact go out. They were to make disciples. You see, the Lord had it all planned. He realized that the disciples were going to have a tendency to settle in Jerusalem and create quite a fellowship at home. They were going to build the Jerusalem First Baptyterian Church and run buses all over the outlying area in order to produce one grand Christian fellowship—but the Lord had other ideas. He had the necessary persecution all lined up, and when the time was right He was going to allow that persecution to fall on the church like a large rock falling into a pile of burning embers. Instead of putting out the fire, the rock only causes more fire by scattering the embers, and in the same way the Lord intended to do some scattering. When the believers scattered, what were they to do? Make disciples, baptize, propagate. But that is direction. That is instruction. That is not the call!

Where then is the call to be found in the Scriptures? There are various passages having to do with the call, but perhaps none is better known than Romans 12. At least none is better known than the first two verses of chapter 12. It is my conviction that if the church were as familiar with the rest of Romans 12 as it is with the first two verses, we would be much further along in the fulfilling of the Great Commission. But we will have to start with verses 1 and 2. These two verses sum up the entire scriptural teaching on the matter of the call.

> I beseech you therefore, brethren, by the mercies of God, that ye present your bodies a living sacrifice, holy, acceptable unto God, which is your reasonable service. And be not conformed to this world: but be ye transformed by the renewing of your mind, that ye may prove what is that good, and acceptable, and perfect, will of God.

My pastor, Dr. R. S. Beal, who for fifty-two years was the pastor of the large First Baptist Church of Tucson, Arizona, used to say, "When you find the word 'therefore' in the Word of God, stop and see what it is there for!" And the "therefore" in Romans 12:1 is there for a purpose. It is there to refer us back over the contents of the preceding eleven chapters. Paul starts out by giving us a picture of man as he rejected the message God had given to His creation. In Romans 1:18 he tells us that "the wrath of God is revealed from heaven against all ungodliness and unrighteousness of men, who suppress the truth in unrighteousness" (NASB). He then goes on to describe how man sank lower and lower into all forms of depravity. It is here that we find the beginnings of homosexuality and lesbianism and all the other moral decay that is so evident in our country today. But we are not left with simply a descriptive picture of what happens to natural man when he rejects God. Paul goes on to show how all mankind is born in sin and that the end result of sin is death, eternal separation from a holy and loving God. He goes on in Romans 3 and 4 to explain God's plan for justifying sinners and tells us in Romans 5:1 that when we are justified through faith in Jesus Christ, one of the results is peace with God. But the believer soon discovers that he still has the nature with which he was born and he longs to have victory over it. In chapters 6, 7, and 8 Paul explains how victory is possible and tells about the Spirit of God, who comes to indwell every believer and to help every believer in every area of his life. We are assured that God has a plan for each life and that He works out everything for His glory in the life of the believer. He takes a few more chapters to explain that God has chosen to bless all nations via His chosen people Israel, but that the Jews as a nation turned their backs on God and God set them aside for a time. Paul shares his deep burden for his own people in chapters 9, 10, and 11, making it very clear in 11:26 that Israel is going to be saved. But now we come to 12:1 and Paul says: "Therefore—because of all I have written up to this point, because of all that God has done for you—I beseech you—you! You, who were not of the chosen race, but who have now been chosen in Christ. You who have been saved and drawn into a family relationship with God. You who deserved death and hell and God's full wrath. I command you to make a sacrifice, a living sacrifice. A living sacrifice of yourself!" That is the call, the only call besides that of soverign election to be found in the Word of God, and it applies to every born-again believer, man or woman, boy or girl, red or yellow, black or white.

It is interesting that Paul calls for a sacrifice, and I am confident that his use of the word held far more meaning for the believers in the early church than it does for us today, for they were all still familiar with the old Jewish custom of offering sacrifices. The term "living sacrifice" certainly caught their attention, for up to that time they had only thought in terms of dead sacrifices. Sacrifice meant taking the life of the creature being sacrificed, and although Paul was applying the word in a new manner, he still was calling for death—death to self, death to self's ambitions, desires, plans, yes, death to everything in the believer which was normally under the control of the prince of the power of the air. Verse 2 goes on to describe how the death was to take place, but the word "living" in verse 1 makes it clear that the call was for the believer to present his living body to the risen Christ so that He could have a vessel through which to do His work.

The rest of Romans 12 goes on to explain how the risen Christ wants to take the living sacrifices, which have been emptied of self, and fill them with *Himself*. In doing this He gives to different "bodies" different abilities and responsibilities. We refer to these as gifts, and every one of these gifts is necessary for the construction of the church, which Jesus Christ *Himself* is building. Preachers, teachers, evangelists, missionaries, carpenters, plumbers, ranchers, doctors, housewives, poets, songwriters, truck drivers, policemen, pilots, judges, schoolteachers, businessmen, executives, salesmen, and so on—all are important.

Up to this point I rather suspect that most of you are still with me. If you have been in Christian circles a few years, you have most likely heard all of this and you probably agree with all of it. So what is the problem? The problem is that the average Christian has read it, has heard it, has memorized it, has accepted it, has believed it, has professed it, and, yes, has even proclaimed it, without ever having put it into practice. The average Christian, if he has made any attempt at all to put Romans 12:1-2 into practice, has only done so mentally and then only in a few specific areas of his life. Notice that I said, "the average Christian." You may be well above average, so you should not become angry with me and feel that I am talking about you personally. But the fact that the laborers are still few when at the same time hundreds of fine evangelical churches in America and around the world are filled to overflowing certainly indicates that the average believer is still not facing up to the real meaning of the "call."

Let me ask some questions. Are you a born-again believer? (There really is no other kind, but I trust you know what I mean.) Do you recognize that as a believer in Jesus Christ you have been called of God to present your body as a living sacrifice? Have you responded to that call? If you are a student, what school are you attending? What are you studying? Why are you attending that school? Why are you studying that course? If you are out of school, what is your work? Why are you working in your particular job? Now if we ask these questions, and we often do, of the preacher or the missionary, we expect him to be able to tell us about his "call" to his work. Why are the preacher and the missionary in a special class all by themselves? Why do you think they get to have that special "call" and the rest of the body of believers do not? Do you see what I am driving at? What we refer to as a "call" is not that at all. It is direction. And every believer who responds to the call of God for a living sacrifice receives direction. We trust that the preacher or the missionary received some definite direction before entering the ministry or the mission field. (Unfortunately, some have misread the directions, but that is another story.) But what about you? Perhaps God has not directed you into the full-time pastorate or into being a full-time missionary in the professional sense of the term, but can you say that He has directed you into your present work? Can you point to His direction for studying what you are studying? Have you responded to God's call for your body as a living sacrifice? Are you directed of God? If not, then please excuse me for saying it, but you are, after all, one of those average Christians I spoke of earlier. And you are part of the reason the laborers are few.

Going back to Romans 12:2, there is a way for you and me to know what God wants us to be doing and where He wants us to be doing it. When the child of God allows the Spirit of God to take the Word of God and apply it to himself, the mind of that child is transformed, renewed. When that takes place, the child of God finds himself able to confirm just what God's will is for his life. God has a will for every life. He has a will in relation to the believer's life partner, but, unfortunately, many, many Christians never discovered what that will was because they never came to the place of allowing the Spirit of God to renew their minds. Many Christians are not really happy or fulfilled in their businesses—because they never

stopped to seek His will before getting into those businesses.

On the other hand (and forgive me for having dwelt on
the negative for so long), there are scores of men and
women in the church of Jesus Christ today who are excited about being in the center of His will in the professional or business world, on the farm or ranch, in the arts
and sciences, in the classroom, and even in retirement. (I
believe that for the real believer there may be a physical
age when human laws require he quit the job, but there is
no mandatory spiritual retirement age. When God gets
ready to retire His workers, He calls them home.) Just
recently I received a letter from a dear friend, a carpenter
called and directed of God, who has come to understand
the reality of that which we are considering here. A
number of years ago, while visiting in his home, I had an
opportunity to tell him about some needs we had in Japan
for a dedicated carpenter. We were developing a year-
around camping ministry in northern Japan in coopera-
tion with our association of Baptist churches, but the
economic situation at that time made it impossible for us
to have the building done commercially. Our first building came into being when a group of dedicated Christian
men who had responded to the call of God were directed
of the Lord to come over and help us. We were now ready
for another building, and when I showed some pictures
and explained to my new carpenter friend the need, he
and his wife made it a matter of prayer, and God showed
them His will. She remained at home and cared for the
family and the family business while he flew to Japan and
used his abilities for the Lord. That family has never been
the same since. The husband and wife have been serving
the Lord in various places both in and out of the United
States, and, as this is being written, they are both in

Arabia on yet another short-term ministry. In the letter I just received from them, he wrote:

> The thought of going into a hot climate doesn't exactly turn me on, but what *does* excite me is the way God replies when you say, "Here I am, Lord, use me!" I've said that many times and each time I have had the opportunity to serve, it's been a special blessing to me. Then the way He gives the extra strength and extra encouragement when each task is undertaken!!!

It has been my privilege to get to know many people like those two over the years. Some came to help in various ways with the ministry of the missionaries in Japan. One dear lady, who had retired after serving as a bookkeeper and executive secretary in a large lumber company in Oregon, came to Japan to assist the missionaries by relieving them of secretarial and bookkeeping responsibilities for which they were not trained, allowing them to give more time to the work for which they had been trained. An eye condition made it necessary for her to return to the States for surgery, but she still wants to return to Japan. In a recent letter she said, "My time in Japan was the happiest time of my life!"

In the building projects referred to above, the assistant director of The Firs Bible and Missionary Conference in Bellingham, Washington, a man who is a real jack-of-all-trades, came to help on three occasions. A seventy-five year young retired schoolteacher came with him. Then there were a young building contractor, a sixty-five year old retired cement finisher, and a young plumber. They all had three things in common: (1) They were not in the "full-time professional ministry," (2) They had all responded to the call of God upon their lives, (3) They all discovered the perfect will of God for at least one short period of their lives.

Have you ever heard the story of the young Marine recruit on the drill field for the first time? All the men in his squad were standing at parade rest when the drill sergeant bellowed out, "Ten-shun!"

Everybody snapped to attention, waiting for the next order. Then came the command, "Forward, march!" Everybody stepped out—everybody, that is, except the young recruit to whom I refer. The sarge couldn't believe his eyes. He brought the squad to a halt and walked over to the young fellow, who was still standing at attention. Grabbing his right ear with one hand, the sergeant put his mouth down close to it and yelled, "Hey, fellow, does this thing work?"

"Yes, sir," came the reply.

The sergeant then marched around to the left side, grabbed that ear and again yelled, "How about this one? Is it working?"

Again the reply, "Yes, sir!"

"Did you hear me say, 'Forward, march'?"

"Yes, sir!"

"Then why in the world didn't you move out with the rest of the squad?"

The young fellow responded in amazement, "Oh, did you mean me, sir? I didn't hear my name."

Well, of course you and I hope that this is only a story, for we would hate to think of what a Marine sergeant would say or do to a fellow like that. But isn't that exactly the way many soldiers of the cross are acting today? Our Commander in Chief has given to His church the command "Forward, march," and while many of the troops are singing things like, "Where He leads me I will follow," or "Anywhere with Jesus," or "To the work, to the work," or any of a dozen other such hymns, the laborers are still few. Many are saying, "If He calls me, I will gladly follow."

Well, if you are saying that, I have news for you. If you are a child of God, you have been called. Your orders are in and waiting for you. The call is there in Romans 12:1, and the directions will come through loud and clear when you get your heart and mind tuned in on His wavelength. God has a special job just for you, a job for which He has given you some equipment and for which He will someday ask you for an accounting.

Paul tells us in Romans 12 a little about some of that special equipment the Lord gives to His workers, and while he does not specifically mention all the various kinds of equipment, he does speak of several for the sake of illustration. He says in verse 4 that we do not all get the same equipment:

> We have many members in one body, and all members have not the same office.

And in verse 3 he says that God passes the equipment out as He sees fit:

> For I say, through the grace given unto me, to every man that is among you, not to think of himself more highly than he ought to think; but to think soberly, according as God hath dealt to every man the measure of faith.

Some get equipped for preaching, others for teaching. There is equipment for exhortation. But notice especially verse 8, where Paul speaks about the equipment for giving:

> He that giveth, let him do it with simplicity.

And tie in verse 11, where Paul tells those who get the equipment for giving how to use it:

> Not slothful in business; fervent in spirit; serving the
> Lord.

Paul must have thought that this was an especially important bit of equipment, for he also directs verse 13 to the same subject:

> Distributing to the necessity of saints; given to hospitality.

Mr. Businessman, Mr. Executive, have you ever faced up to the possibility that God gave you the equipment you possess, not just for your personal needs, but for the building of His church? Perhaps you have faithfully been giving the Lord a percentage of what you make in the business world, but what if the preacher or missionary only gave the same percentage of his time and effort? If, in fact, we are all called of God to present ourselves as living sacrifices, it is evident that many of us need to rethink a great many details of our lives. One of the reasons the laborers are still few is because Satan has been successful in fooling many believers, causing them to think that the "call" is something that pertains to preachers and missionaries only, and that the rest of God's people have no need for such an "experience."

The psalmist, in writing about the experiences of Israel, makes a very interesting observation in Psalm 106:15, where he states,

> And he gave them their request; but sent leanness into
> their soul.

Is it not still so today as far as much of the church is concerned? How often do we hear God's people pointing to the material possessions, their fine houses, their new cars, their high-paying jobs, as indications of the blessing of the Lord upon them, while at the same time there is a shallowness to their lives? The continual push for bigger and better houses, finer furnishings, bigger bank ac-

counts, and so on points up quite glaringly the lack of
inner peace and satisfaction, the lack of a sense of the call
for a living sacrifice which should mark every child of
God. Yes, perhaps it can be said that the material blessings are from the Lord, but only in the same way that
those Israelites were granted their requests: material
prosperity with spiritual poverty.

God saved you for a purpose. Jesus Christ bought you
for a purpose. He has a beautiful plan for your life, a
special function, a special place of service in His overall
program of building His body, the church, and He yearns
for you to respond to His call for the living sacrifice of
your body so that He can give you His directions. If anything in your life is of greater importance to you than
Jesus Christ and His program, you can be sure that when
you respond to His call for your body He is going to put
His hand on that particular treasure which is more important to you than He Himself is. It will have to go, for Jesus
Christ will accept no rivals in the lives of His own. If your
social position in life is more important to you than God's
program, you can be sure that a full surrender to Jesus
Christ will cost you that social position. If, on the other
hand, Jesus Christ rules supreme in your life, it is very
possible that your high social position is something He
will use and bless for His own honor and glory. After all,
when this life is over, that high social position will result
in no eternal benefits unless it was used for His glory.

Jesus Christ said that He was going to build His church,
and that is exactly what He is doing today. That church
will be completed on schedule whether you and I get
involved or not. His work is not going to suffer because
we fail to get involved. It is so sad the way we can twist
the facts all around and come up with the wrong conclusions. Jesus Christ is not begging for your help. He is

offering you the privilege of having a share in what He is doing. He is not in need of your time, your money, your efforts. The cattle on a thousand hills are His, and the wealth of every field is His. He is able to sell some of His cows anytime He wants to and come up with all the money He needs. But He wants you and me to become partners with Him in His work so that we might reap the eternal dividends He has provided for us. And often, when one of His own responds to the call to give his body as a living sacrifice, Jesus Christ will give him one of His oil wells or a gold mine or the cattle ranch to manage for Him.

Every gift, every talent, every ability you have, you received from God. It is not yours, it is His, and the day is coming when you will be called before Him to give an account of your stewardship. If you insist on using what God has given to you for your own enjoyment, God well may grant you your desire. But I can assure you, on the authority of the Word of God, that the judgment seat of Jesus Christ will reveal to all that you were the loser. Let's quit kidding ourselves about the call. You, too, have been called of God, to present your living body to Him, and God wants desperately to direct you in paths of usefulness and blessing, if and when you will respond to that call.

4

Let's Quit Kidding Ourselves About The Command

THE PARABLE OF THE APPLE PICKERS

Once upon a time there was an apple grower who had acres and acres of apple orchards. One day he went to the village, contracted for 1,000 apple pickers, and charged them with their responsibilities. He said to them, "I want you to go out into all my orchards and harvest the ripe apples, building storage facilities for them so that they will not spoil. I will provide all you will need to complete the task, and I will reward you according to your faithfulness when I return. As a group you will be responsible for the entire operation, but, naturally, all of you will not be able to do the actual harvesting, as some will be engaged in carrying supplies, others in caring for the physical needs of the group, and still others in administrative responsibilities."

He then gave specific instructions to various individuals, making some pickers, and others packers, and others truck drivers, and administrators, and cooks, and accountants, and storehouse builders, and apple inspectors. Although everybody could pick apples, 100 were designated as full-time pickers.

In all, the apple grower had 10,000 acres of trees, and the 100 pickers started out at once to begin their harvesting work. Ninety-four of the pickers started picking right around the homestead, while 6 packed up a few supplies and headed out to the orchards many miles away.

In time, the 800 acres immediately surrounding the homestead blossomed with apple storehouses filled to overflowing with beautiful apples, and the orchards on those acres boasted thousands of apple trees almost picked bare. In fact, the ninety-four apple pickers working in those 800 acres were having more and more difficulty finding apples to pick, so, having time on their hands, they decided to put more effort into building larger storehouses and developing better equipment for picking and packing their apples. Although there were yet apples to be picked from trees on the central 800 acres—here and there were small orchards in some rugged country a bit more difficult to reach where the trees still had large crops to be harvested—apples by the tens of thousands were rotting and falling to the ground on the remaining 9,200 acres because the six pickers sent out to work those fields were simply not able to gather all the fruit that was ripe.

From time to time some of the full-time pickers passed away, but back at the homestead members of the Society for the Picking of Apples were faithfully producing more prospective pickers, and they had a number of schools that specialized in training apple pickers. One day a prospective apple-picking student proved to have some special talents for picking quickly and effectively, and when he heard of the thousands of acres of yet untouched orchards he began thinking and talking of heading out into one of those faraway orchards. But some of his friends began to discourage him by saying, "With all your talent and ability, you would be far more valuable here around the homestead. Why, you could help to harvest apples from the trees on our central 800 acres more rapidly and give all of us that much more time to build bigger and better storehouses, and perhaps you could even help us devise better ways to use our big storehouses since we have more space than we need for the present crop of apples."

Trouble soon developed among the ninety-four pickers around the homestead. Some began stealing apples that had already been picked, and although there were still enough trees even on the 800 acres for all the available workers, some began fighting among and even in the trees. Some living on the northern edge of the homestead began sending their trucks to haul off apples from the southern side, and those on the south side sent their trucks to gather on the east side. Even stranger yet, near each of the apple pickers' homes were trees that were for one reason or another a bit more difficult to work. The apples were harder to get off, requiring a bit more time and effort, and the Society for the Picking of Apples hit upon a plan whereby the members of the society living in the east end of the homestead would send special pickers to those difficult trees in the west side, and those in the west side would send pickers to the difficult trees in the east side.

With so many workers and so few trees, the pickers and packers and truck drivers—and all the rest of the Society for the Picking of Apples living on the homestead—had lots of time for things other than just picking apples, so they began building nice houses and making a better life for themselves. They were very conscious of the proper styles of dress, and when the six pickers from the far-off orchards returned to the homestead for a visit, it was evident that they had not kept up with the styles. But those on the homestead were always good to the six, and they always gave them the red-carpet treatment. Nevertheless, somehow or other those six always had a difficult time understanding why the Society for the Picking of Apples continued to designate 96 percent of the budget for bigger and better apple-picking methods and equipment and personnel for the 800 acres around the homestead and only 4 percent for the really ripe orchards out in the distance. The six knew that an apple is an apple wherever it may be picked and that the apples around the homestead were just as important as apples far away, but somehow or other they could not erase from their minds the tens of thousands of trees away out there which had never been picked, They longed for some pickers, and packers, and truck drivers, and supervisors, and equipment-maintenance men, and ladder builders, yes, and even some professionals to teach better apple-picking methods out there where the apples were falling and rotting on the ground. Somehow or other they had in their hearts the nagging question of whether or not the people in the Society for the Picking of Apples were really majoring on the task assigned to them by the owner of the orchards.

There were those, of course, who were convinced that apple picking requires the best of equipment, so they were developing bigger and better ladders and nicer boxes in which to store the apples, and they raised the standard of qualifications for full-time apple pickers. But when the owner returns and sees the acres of untouched apples, I wonder how happy he will be about the bigger and better ladders.

Beloved, lets quit kidding ourselves about the command.

In spite of all that has been written about the command and the call in relation to missions, there still remains much confusion. The call, the command, and direction are all different. The call comes to all believers, all are called of God to give themselves entirely to Him for His service. We, as a redeemed people, are no longer to be of this world. We are pilgrims and strangers dedicated to God, and we are constantly warned in the Scriptures not to become entangled with the things of this world.

> No man that warreth entangleth himself with the affairs of this life; that he may please him who hath chosen him to be a soldier [2 Tim. 2:4].

All those who name the name of Jesus Christ are called to be soldiers of Jesus Christ. That is the call.

We have also seen that when we respond to the call of God for our lives, our Commander in Chief then comes through with specific direction for each individual soldier. He directs one into the medical profession, another into the teaching profession, another into business. The thrilling thing is that God has a unique plan for the life of every one of His children, and He will give direction for every detail if His children desire such direction. But just as the believer is free to reject the call of God for his body, so he is free to ignore the directions God has for him.

But what about the command? What about that thing we refer to as "the Great Commission?" Perhaps I can illustrate it in this way. A nation finds it necessary to go to war with another nation. A call is sent out for *all* citizens to give themselves for the war effort. Those who respond to the call are then divided into different categories.

Some are qualified to bear arms and go out to do the actual fighting, while others are sent to work in the factories, the mines, the fields. Some are asked to make the guns and the uniforms, others to grow the necessary food. Some train the fighting men, others handle logistics, planning, finance, or research and development of new weapons. Which of those we have mentioned can we do without? None, of course. All are important to the war effort. Now, what is the call, what is the command, and what is direction? The call, which goes out to everyone, is for the people to give themselves for the war effort. The direction is that which determines what each individual is going to be doing in the overall program. And the command is the actual commission to go to war.

Notice a very important fact at this point, for it is here that many become confused. The command, in this case, is to wage war with the enemy, and this command is not to an individual but to an entire nation. In our apple-picking parable the command to go out and harvest 10,000 acres of apples was not to individuals as such, but to the entire Society for the Picking of Apples. In order to obey that command the society had to have ladder builders and truckers and teachers and a host of support facilities. The command was to go out into all the orchards and gather apples, an impossibility for the individual, but a real option for the society. In the same way, our Commander in Chief has given His church a command. That command is, "Therefore go and make disciples of all nations, baptizing them in the name of the Father and of the Son and of the Holy Spirit, and teaching them to obey everything I have commanded you" (Matt. 28:19-20, NIV).

That command, if taken as a command to an individual, is an absolute impossibility. There is no way that I, as an

individual, can possibly go into all the world and preach
the gospel, nor is it intended that I should attempt to do
so. It is here where the great teaching relative to the body
of Christ is so important, for it was to His body that Christ
gave the great commission—the command to get the
message out to the entire world and make disciples. That
body has many members, and each member has a different function. But (and I emphasize that conjunction) the
problem is that too many within that body today relegate
the command to just a few members of the body. Our
God-given command is to be witnesses to the entire
world, and the contention I am making is that, like those
in the parable of the apple pickers, a large segment of the
body of Christ is busily engaged in fulfilling part of the
command on only a small part of the field, and confusion
abounds on every hand. In other words, we are kidding
ourselves about the command for missions.

The church is instructed to go, to pray, to give; and it is
only as the body of Christ operates as a body, each
member fulfilling his responsibility, that the job gets
done. We all cannot go personally to a foreign field, but
the church can go as it sends some of its members. And
every member does become a part of the whole as he
"goes" right where he is. We all can give to some degree,
but there are those whom God has blessed with greater
financial resources, and it is His intention that those
greater resources be used for the sending program of the
church.

Acts 13 is a thrilling example of this very principle at
work in the New Testament church. The church was not
waiting for some individual to volunteer. The believers
were sensitive to the leading of the Holy Spirit, and they
sent the best-qualified men they had. They knew what the
command was, and the carrying out of that command

became their number one objective. There is a great deal of talk about "majoring in missions" among us today, but the phrase "minoring in missions" might be closer to the truth, and possibly "dabbling" would be even closer to the facts. I know that some are going to find fault with this statement, but look at the facts. When 94 percent of the seminary graduates today are going out to pick apples in just 6 percent of the orchard, are we majoring, minoring, or dabbling? When 96 percent of church income is being used in the ministries and programs dealing with 6 percent, and just 4 percent is being used to reach out into the rest of the orchard, are we majoring, minoring, or dabbling? When veteran missionaries in various places around the world are telling of great influxes of new converts and of their total inabililty to meet the challenge for discipling and church planting because of a lack of workers and, at the same time, back on the homestead, the graduate schools for apple pickers are sending out letters asking if anybody knows of opportunities for their upcoming graduates—are we majoring, minoring, or dabbling? When God's people are living in beautiful houses, driving expensive automobiles, building heated swimming pools, and otherwise enjoying some of the material blessings of the richest nation on earth, and, at the same time, when the few who are ready and willing to head out to the "orchards out back" must take twelve, eighteen, or twenty-four months to get the necessary financial support, I ask again, are we majoring, minoring or simply dabbling in missions?

I believe that there are a number of ways in which we are kidding ourselves about the command. In the first place, we have fooled ourselves into thinking that the Great Commission is for the missionary, the ones who "feel called" to leave this country and go to preach in a distant land. And we further fool ourselves by thinking that this type of work is only for the professionally trained theological student. The fact of the matter is that there are some very needy places around the world where the doors are closed to the professional missionary but open to the nonprofessional missionary. I think of the Christian Chiropractic Association, a group of Christian chiropractors who sponsor Christian nationals from some "closed door" countries through chiropractic schools in the States and then send them back to their native countries to witness for the Lord Jesus Christ. The nationals earn their own living, not by making tents as Paul did, but by their practice of chiropractic.

We kid ourselves about the command when we use it to justify much activity not envisioned by the command at all. Had the apple pickers in our parable started picking mushrooms, nobody could say that they were doing something wrong, but they were not fulfilling the command to pick apples when they were picking mushrooms. Mushrooms, as good as they may be, are simply not apples. Now, if they were picking the mushrooms in order to provide something to nourish themselves with so that in turn they would have the physical strength to pick more apples, we can see the validity of picking mushrooms. The command to the church is to go out into all the world and disciple the nations, establishing groups of believers in every place so that those groups can in turn join in the overall task, reaching yet others. Planting churches—and by that term I mean evangelizing, training the converts resulting from the evangelizing, and organizing them into local bodies of believers with officers and leaders as set forth in the New Testament—and starting orphanages are not the same! Planting churches and starting schools are not the same. Planting churches and carrying on litera-

ture programs are not the same. And only as the mush-
room picking can be shown to be a direct aid to the picking of apples should the members of the Society for
Apple Picking allow themselves to be so engaged.
Otherwise, they are kidding themselves about the command.

The command is that we move forward. The command
is that we attack. The command is that we move out and
conquer. In other words, we are at war. Jesus Christ has
declared war on Satan and all his forces, and every believer has been called of God to join the battle. Notice the
emphasis in the Word:

> Watch ye, stand fast in the faith, quit you like men, be
> strong [1 Cor. 16:13].
> Wherefore take unto you the whole armour of God: . . . the
> shield . . . the helmet . . . the sword [Eph. 6:13, 16-17].
> This charge I commit unto thee, son Timothy . . . that
> thou by them mightest war a good warfare [1 Tim. 1:18].
> Fight the good fight of faith [1 Tim. 6:12].
> No man that warreth entangleth himself with the affairs of
> this life; that he may please him who hath chosen him to
> be a soldier [2 Tim. 2:4].

These are but a few of the many passages that could be
cited to show that we have been commanded to do battle.
The terminology of warfare is used consistently throughout Scripture, and one would have to be blind to miss it.

At this point it would seem very fitting to consider the
warning of Amos in Amos 6:1:

> Woe to them that are at ease in Zion. [That is, Woe to the
> people of God who are at ease!]

Are you at ease? Is your local church at ease? Is there
anything about your way of life, your business, your style

of living which would indicate that you are involved in a war?

The stories of Israel are filled with illustrations for us today. The command to the children of Israel was that they were to move out and take possession of the land God had promised them, but they only partially obeyed. It was God's desire that they have it all, and He promised to make them victorious if they would only obey Him.

The church has likewise been commanded to move out and into the world to conquer it for Jesus Christ. He has again promised victory if we are obedient. He has promised His presence, His provision, His peace. And the Scriptures abound with illustrations of the day when He will return for an accounting of our faithfulness.

How sad that the only battles many Christians have engaged in are battles with self and with other Christians. Are you in His army? Are you desirous of being a soldier of Jesus Christ? Are you involved in "the affairs of this life"? The command is a call to action, a call to war, and I am convinced that the church as a whole is kidding itself about that command. There is a burning world to be conquered for Jesus Christ, and we are playing games in our own back yard. I am constrained to ask, If the church of Jesus Christ were obeying the commands of its Commander in Chief today, if the local church were doing what the Scriptures indicate it should be doing, would there really be the need for mission societies to be involved in the interurban ministries as we have them today?

Praise God for the home mission societies and the interurban ministries they are carrying on, because the local church has not obeyed the commands. But the church is in Chicago. The church is in New York. The church is in Denver. Why do we need interurban missionaries? Because the church has failed to pick the apples in one section of its own backyard, leaving a cluster of trees for some "specialists" from another area to come and harvest. On the local level we work with the people living in the inner city, we go to school with them, we ride buses with them, we attend ball games with them, we have all kinds of contacts with them, but when it comes to reaching them for Jesus Christ, we have to call in the specialized apple pickers. Who is kidding whom?

Again I ask, Are we at ease in Zion? Are you aware of the fact that the church has been commanded to reach a lost and dying world and that you are a vital part of that church? Are you aware of the fact that Jesus Christ came to seek and to save the lost—and that while there still are many lost among the 6 percent of the North American continent, by far the greater portion of the lost are out in the regions beyond? And are you aware of the fact that the church in America is primarily focused on the 6 percent—and the fact that you and I are part of that American church, so we share the responsibility? Beloved, let's quit kidding ourselves about the command.

5

Let's Quit Kidding Ourselves About The Finances

As the material for this book was being reviewed prior to publication, I was told by an official of a large mission board that I was "rocking the boat" with some of my presentations on finances. It is not my intention to be sensational, nor do I enjoy being in a position where many of those whom I love and respect seem to be advising me to tone down a message I honestly believe the Lord has laid upon my heart. The message presented in this chapter is not a popular one, and it is quite possible that it will call forth a great deal of rebuttal on the part of those who feel endangered by a "rocking of the boat." However, if what I have written can in any way raise questions, either publicly or privately, which will cause Christians to delve into the Word of God for some answers to some important financial questions, I will praise the Lord for the opportunity to "rock the boat."

I have no degree in economics nor do I make any claim to special revelation in this or any other area. It is simply that Psalm 1:1 keeps ringing in my heart—"Blessed is the man that walketh not in the counsel of the ungodly"— and I wonder if many of God's people are not doing just exactly that when it comes to financial matters. If what I have written causes my readers to search the Scriptures seriously in relation to their financial dealings, whether they come to the same conclusions I have or come up with distinctly different ones, I will consider my time and effort well spent. My whole purpose is to challenge people, God's people, to make the kind of investments which will result in greater eternal dividends. It is my conviction that many well-meaning Christians are kidding themselves about this whole matter of stewardship.

The apostle Paul urged the Corinthians to examine themselves to see if they were indeed in the faith. Some things going on in that church gave the apostle reason to wonder about some of the people. In the same way, it seems to me that some things going on in Christian circles today in the area of finances give us ample reason to cry out, "Examine yourselves and your policies to see if you are on scriptural ground." If, after such examination, you are satisfied that you are on good scriptural ground, that is fine. If the Holy Spirit uses what I have written to bring about a change in your financial policies, thereby bringing you greater eternal dividends, I will rejoice with you.

I simply desire to set forth a point of view that in our day has few vocal proponents. The careful reader will quickly notice that I raise some questions for which I give no answers. The reason for this is quite simple—I do not have the answers. I do not know the specifics of God's plan and program for your life—what kind of house you should live in, what kind of car you should drive, how you should divide up your monthly budget—these you must determine for yourself. But God has given us some definite principles in His Word, and it is for these that we will be held responsible. It is my hope and prayer that you are not kidding yourself about those principles.

As I turn to the subject of finances, I am inclined to start with another parable.

A TWENTIETH-CENTURY PARABLE

And He called unto Himself His created ones and divided unto them as He saw fit. To one He gave a ranch in the beautiful high country of Colorado, with much cattle and thousands of acres of lush pasture land. To another He gave some oil wells in the vast plains of Texas. To a third He gave much stock in various business enterprises around the world, and to yet others He gave special genius to create beautiful music and art and to originate beautiful new designs for buildings and parks and cities. To some He gave the ability to write good books and to make things plain to the minds of other men. These He called teachers. There were yet others to whom He gave little material wealth, but these He blessed with strong backs and good health and the ability to use both in productive ways.

In His wisdom, the Creator gave to some of His creatures special gifts that other created ones would not recognize as gifts or blessings. To some He gave broken bodies, blind eyes, or deaf ears. Others received poor health or limited mental abilities, and divided among the masses were different colors of skin, hair, and eyes.

Everything His created ones possessed they received from Him, and not one of them possessed anything that was not received from Him. All was according to His plan and His desire, and the distribution of all things was for His own glory.

And then, to a very small group of His creatures, God gave the most precious of all gifts. He gave them His Book, the Bible. In this Book was complete information for the understanding and management of all the gifts and blessings He had divided among His creatures, and, more than that, in this Book God revealed Himself and His love for all mankind. He invited all men everywhere to partake freely of His great salvation. Also in this Book God made it abundantly clear that on a set day, known only to Himself, He would require a complete audit of the books and the settling of all accounts. The rewards for faithfulness and the penalties for unfaithfulness would be staggering.

To those who were among the privileged few receiving this special gift was also given an awesome responsibility accompanied by some severe warnings. The Book and its message were to be shared with the entire world, for God also loved those who did not have the Book, and He stated clearly that He was not willing that any should go without its message. And truly, those who had this special Book were blessed indeed, for because of its impact they developed hospitals, high standards of morality, higher education, and concepts of human rights and freedoms. Womanhood was given an exalted position, and life took on real meaning.

God said to His creatures, "You are free to use what I have given you in any way you see fit. If you do not want to use what I have given you for My glory, that is up to you. It is all Mine—you had nothing when you entered this life, and you take nothing with you when you leave it—and I can reclaim it at will. However, if you so desire, you may use what I have given to you to build eternal possessions in heaven. You may take nothing from here to there, but you may so manage what I have given to you here in such a way that you lay up real treasures there. Do not, truly I say to you, do not lay up for yourselves treasures here on this earth, for they can only deteriorate or be consumed.

"Be not deceived, many will come to you with this plan or that plan, urging you to amass a fortune, laying up such treasures in their care. They promise you regular interest payments while you remain on earth (and if everything goes according to their economic planning, they should be able to fulfill their promises), but there are some inherent dangers involved. If I direct you to set aside a portion of My provisions to care for your earthly needs in your latter days and you choose to use one of these programs which assure you that after your death the balance of your estate will be used for My glory, then you will be called a wise and faithful servant. Be careful, however, that what you lay up for your old age is reasonable in amount. The tendency is to build up treasures far beyond your needs and to be deceived into thinking that eternal dividends are earned by leaving it all for Me upon your death. Remember what I said to the rich farmer, 'Thou fool, this night thy soul shall be required of thee: then whose shall those things be?' (Luke 12:20). In other words, the instant the farmer died he lost possession of everything. Eternal investments are made while you are living. I have loaned you some of My possessions to use during your lifetime. They are My possessions, not yours, and when your life is ended I will redistribute them according to My will. How foolish to think one can use what I give for one's own personal satisfaction and enjoyment during life and then expect to receive commendation for leaving it for My use after he can no longer use it. Verily, I say unto you, do your depositing in the Bank of Heaven during regular business hours, from birth to death! As some mortal has said, 'How much better to give while you are able to enjoy seeing your gifts at work for the Lord.' Truly those in the early church were wise, for it is written of them that 'as many as were possessors of

lands or houses sold them, and brought the prices of the
things that were sold, and laid them down at the apostles'
feet: and distribution was made unto every man according
as he had need' (Acts 4:34-35). How fortunate that they
never hit upon the idea of tying up all that property in
annuity programs!

"Again I say, be careful that you are not deceived if you
are privileged to live in that place called America, for in
America even the established government will give you
income tax credits for giving up to a certain amount.
Many there are who give just that amount in order to
enjoy such tax credits and at the same time gain a reputa-
tion in the church as generous givers. Verily, they have
their reward. They have gained the reputations they have
sought after, and they also received the desired tax credits. I did not allow Ananias and Sapphira to get away with
that, but not wanting to deplete the church in this day
and age, I will allow men to build such reputations if they
so foolishly choose. If you give because you love Me and
still reap the benefit of a tax break, then you are twice
blessed, for you then have even more with which to
glorify Me. Most of your brothers around the world do not
enjoy this privilege.

"Do not err in thinking that you are rich or especially
blessed because you have received much money and great
possessions. Some who have received far less are much
richer. It is possible to have much and to be rich at the
same time, but it is unusual. It is also possible to have
little and be rich. Such was the widow who gave her two
mites. How sad the man who has much but is himself
poverty stricken. Such was the farmer with great lands
and barns. I called him a fool, for with all his abundance
he failed to make eternal deposits during his lifetime.
Such, too, are many churches. They think that they are

rich because they have much property and fine buildings and many prosperous and influential members. They have three services every Sunday morning, luxurious carpets, padded pews, a marble bapistry, a full-time staff of highly paid, highly trained professionals, and, their greatest pride—for they are missions minded—a missions budget twice the size of any other church in town. They are even annually counted among the top ten givers in missions. Alas, they do not realize that they are wretched, pitiful, poor, blind, and naked, for they focus on what they are giving and doing for Me, while I see what they are keeping and doing for themselves.

"Verily, I say unto you, there will be those who will use what I give to them to build bigger and better houses and justify themselves by saying, 'We need more room to accomodate the church youth group the second Sunday of every month.' Or there will be those who will build extravagant church buildings and justify their actions by saying, 'We live among the affluent, and if we are going to reach them we must build impressive buildings.' Verily, they have ignored the instructions in My Word. They do not understand that it is My intention that the church building be used for worship and fellowship and for meeting the needs of My people. The church building need not appeal to the unbeliever, for the unbeliever is to be reached out in his world. When he comes to know Me and My love for him, then he will be drawn to the church, not because of the building but because of Me. Verily, I say unto you, man's ideas relative to the church building have not had the desired result. Many have been drawn by spacious buildings and comfortable pews, but they still do not know me.

"No, My sole purpose in all of this, My purpose in creating all mankind and in distributing to mankind vari-

ous gifts, possessions, and abilities, is that all mankind
might glorify Me. This you do by obeying My Word, My
commandments. And what is My commandment? That
you take what I have given to you—your health, or sick-
ness, your strong mind or broken body, your physical
wealth or poverty—yea, yourselves as living sacrifices,
and use all you have and take the message of My Word to
that vast portion of My world which does not yet have
that Word, that they, too, might know how to be good
stewards of life, and that they might receive eternal life."

And many who heard this parable went away dis-
gusted, or angry, or unconcerned, because they did not
like the missionary to talk about money.

If you are one of those Christians who do not like to
hear preachers and missionaries talk about money, I
suggest that you skip to the next chapter, for you certainly
will not enjoy the rest of this one. And please do not feel
that you are alone in this, for you are not. Even Jesus
turned some people off when He spoke about material
possessions. On one occasion a young and successful
lawyer came and asked Jesus what he should do to gain
eternal life, and when Jesus told him to dispose of all his
material possessions first and then come and follow Jesus,
the Scriptures tell us that he went away sad, because he
had great wealth. I do not believe that the average Christian today can really understand what that young fellow
went through as he listened to the Lord, for few of us
possess that kind of wealth. If Jesus were to ask us to give
up everything we possess in order to follow Him, that
would not be nearly as difficult a test for us as it was for
the rich young ruler. He had so much, and, the cost of

following Jesus was just too much. For us it would be much simpler; because we have so little we could easily give it up for Him—or could we?

Has there ever been a time, just one time, in your life when you gave a widow's mite? Perhaps you ask, "What is a widow's mite?" Well, in the gospels of Mark and Luke we read of a widow who cast into the offering box two mites, two of the smallest coins there were in those days, and Jesus, comparing her gift with that of some prosperous businessmen, said that she gave far more than any of them, because she gave out of her poverty and she gave all that she had. In the bookkeeping system of the Bank of Glory, that dear lady turned earthly poverty into eternal riches. Have you ever given all that you had?

Let me ask you something. Do you really believe the Word of God when it comes to the scriptural teaching concerning finances? Of course, when it comes to our verbal confession, we have to say that we do believe. After all, to say no to that question would really show us up to be something other than what we want the rest of the church to think we are. But you do not have to answer out loud. Just reply to the question in your heart, where only you and God can hear the reply. Do you really believe? Now, a second question. If I could look over your financial records, your savings account, your bankbook, your safe-deposit box, your cookie jar—if I could see them all, could I possibly see in all of them any indication that you really believe in the financial teachings of God's Word? Well, I grant you that it is not my desire to look over those records, nor is it my business to want to do so, but I feel in a sense that it is my business to challenge God's people to think seriously about these things, for the God who can hear the answer you have given in your heart is able also to see all the records I have mentioned, and a great many more. He sees what you and I give, and He sees what you and I keep for ourselves. He can see under the floor of Achan's tent, and He can see into the hearts of Ananias and Sapphira.

Some years ago I was flying between Tucson and Denver when a rather prosperous-looking gentleman sitting next to me revealed in a conversation that he was an officer in a church in Tucson. I decided to try a little different approach in witnessing to this man, so I started off by asking him about his business in the hope that he would ask me about mine. It worked, and before long he asked what my business was. I replied, "I am an investment counselor for the largest company in the world."

When he asked what that company was, I went on to tell him that my company had branch offices in almost every country in the world." "In fact," I said, "we have branch offices in every country but two, and we may even have them there now, but we are not sure."

Impatiently, he said, "Well, what is the name of your company?"

I replied, "The church of Jesus Christ." Then I went on to point out the fact that the church of Jesus Christ is worldwide today and that there are groups of believers meeting together either publicly or in secret in every country in the world, with the two possible exceptions of Mongolia and the little African country of Mauritania.

Well, he was not much interested in the conversation after that, except he wanted to know why I said I was an investment counselor, and I explained that I was interested in trying to challenge God's people to invest in things that would reap eternal dividends instead of in things that earn only temporal returns. Jesus Himself acted at times as an investment counselor, for He was constantly urging and encouraging His followers to make

the right kind of investments with their time, their possessions, and their lives. As a matter of fact, Jesus said
more about the matter of stewardship than He said about
any other single subject, and much of what He had to say
concerned material possessions.

> Lay not up for yourselves treasures upon earth, where
> moth and rust doth corrupt, and where thieves break
> through and steal: but lay up for yourselves treasures in
> heaven, where neither moth nor rust doth corrupt, and
> where thieves do not break through nor steal: for where
> your treasure is, there will your heart be also [Matt. 6:19-
> 21].
> For what shall it profit a man, if he shall gain the whole
> world, and lose his own soul? [Mark 8:36].
> Give, and it shall be given unto you;...for with the same
> measure that ye mete withal it shall be measured to you
> again [Luke 6:38].
> For a man's life consisteth not in the abundance of the
> things which he possesseth [Luke 12:15].

What did Jesus mean when He said, "Lay not up for
yourselves treasures upon earth?" I am sure that some
well-trained theologian could come up with a nice-
sounding explanation of these verses, causing them to say
something other than what they seem to say on the sur-
face. In fact, I am confident that if somebody were to do
that, it would put a lot of present-day Christian practice in
a better light, for, to put it very bluntly, I have a suspicion
that the average evangelical believer in America today is
completely out of tune with the obvious meaning of
Matthew 6:19-21. If you ask me to back up that statement,
I will refer you to the dozens of Christian periodicals that
come into our homes each month. Have you ever noticed
the difference in emphasis between the Word of God and
the commercial ads in many Christian publications?

Jesus said, "Lay not up for yourselves," and the articles say, "Lay up for yourselves [with us, of course]." Jesus says, "Give," and the articles say, "Loan it to us."

Do not misunderstand what I am trying to say. I am aware of the admonition Paul gave to believers when he wrote to Timothy and said, "But if any provide not for his own, and specially for those of his own house, he hath denied the faith, and is worse than an infidel" (1 Tim. 5:8). God expects us to use the abilities He has given us to provide properly for our families, and much in the book of Proverbs and in the New Testament instructs us to plan wisely for the days ahead. Various illustrations are used from nature to show us the wisdom of this, but let us be on guard against the common philosophy of man which ignores the difference between treasures and provision for tomorrow. There is a vast difference.

I mentioned earlier that there are scriptural principles to which we need to pay attention. One of these is found in Acts 4:34-37, where we read of the early believers' selling houses and land to meet the needs of other believers. The evident principle is that those early believers looked upon their earthly possessions as being something they were to use to meet the present needs of the body of Christ. They felt a responsibility for that day, that generation, and they gave generously. Many applications could be drawn from this, but the most obvious is that there are needs today for which we who name the name of Christ are responsible—needs that involve getting the gospel to over 2 billion people who have never yet heard. God is not going to hold you and me responsible for the millions of the past generations that never heard the gospel, nor will we be held responsible for the millions that may go untold in the generations to come, providing our disobedience today is not the cause of their not hearing.

We are responsible, however, for the present generation, the present needs. If that school or that Christian organization in which you are interested is doing a good job for the Lord and you desire to support it, fine. Do so generously. But do it now with that which God has given to you. I have already suggested earlier that wise planning might involve you in some kind of deferred-giving program whereby you can provide for your financial needs during your retirement years, but I am constrained to point out some real dangers in this area.

First of all, there is the danger of plain, simple materialism—the danger of putting too much stress on what we think are needs. I recall hearing recently of a woman who wrote to her congressman that she was finding it very difficult to keep up with the taxes on her two cars, her big house, the family camper, a boat, the summer cottage at the lake, and now dog licenses for all three of her dogs!

Another danger is one that I do not believe I have ever heard anyone speak about. But the fact is that institutions historically move away from a scripturally founded position. Man changes and times change. Japan today has a number of prestigious educational institutions that were started years ago as sound evangelical schools, outreaches of evangelical denominations in the United States and Europe. As a matter of fact, there are many similar universities in the United States today—schools that were brought into being to train men and women in the various sciences from a Christian point of view. Millions of dollars from well-to-do Christians and Christian foundations financed the beginnings of those schools. But where are those schools today? Many of them are still enjoying the benefits of financial endowments established by Christians of past generations while at the same time they are doing everything possible to destroy the very Christian principles that brought them into existence. I know of a theological school in America today that has long since betrayed the evangelical position of its founders but is still profiting greatly from the endowments set up by those founders and others of like faith and practice. I would like to think that the Christian organizations (Bible schools, colleges, seminaries, and mission boards) to which I presently contribute will never depart from the faith, but in spite of all the precautions man may take, the heart is still deceitful above all things and desperately wicked. Those institutions are presently dependent upon God's people for their day-to-day operation, and I believe that that is the way it should be. Let those of us who have a measure of His possessions use those possessions to support His work now, today, and let us not be guilty of keeping back for ourselves and our own personal use that which God has given to us to use for His work, thinking that simply leaving it earmarked for some Christian organization after our death will put us into the category of faithful stewards.

Can you imagine what the Lord would have said to one of the servants to whom He had given some of the talents if, upon His return, that servant had told Him, "Lord, I haven't used that money for You yet, but I have arranged for it to be given to a wonderful mission board when I die"? No, I can't even imagine the unfaithful servant's trying to get away with that—but how many are doing just that today?

In the few months since I have returned to the States from Japan I have seen the cost of supporting a missionary to Japan jump almost 16 percent, and this has been going on for several years. Some missionaries have had to come back to the States because they could not secure

sufficient support, and I know of many who are not receiving sufficient salaries or work funds to carry on effectively. And that is just one mission field! The thought has
recently come to me, Is it possible that the Lord is allowing costs to rise so sharply simply to test His servants? Is
it possible that He is wanting to see if we are willing to
match our professions with our possessions?—willing to,
as a very earthy expression puts it, put our money where
our mouth is?

Yes, I am afraid that there is a real danger of annuities
and deferred giving programs bringing us a false sense of
peace and self-satisfaction, making us feel that we are
being good stewards when in actuality we are avoiding
our responsibilities. If you know that a loved one has a
desperate need now, would you feel that you were meeting your responsibility by simply telling him you were
going to leave him $1,000 in your will? He might die
before you do! No, if you felt real love and compassion,
you would help him now, and, by the same token, if you
are really in love with Jesus Christ, you will use what you
have for His glory now and trust Him to make ample
provision for tomorrow.

The real problem confronting us at this point is the lack
of focus on eternity. We talk about heaven, the glory land,
and eternity a great deal as Christians, but somehow we
see little evidence of Christians really being focused in
that direction. How often I think back to those early years
right after the Second World War. When I first went to
Japan back in the early fifties, much of downtown Tokyo
was still in devastation. The rubble had been cleaned up
quickly, but signs of war were all around and poverty was
the obvious fact. Some missions and missionaries were
quick to purchase properties, some right in the heart of
the various business districts. A missionary friend pur-

chased a large Japanese estate that included a big house, a fireproof storehouse, and a huge and beautiful garden— for just $3,000! A few years later that same property was worth up in the six figures, and today that same property would probably make its owner a millionaire. How often I have thought to myself, *Oh, if I had only realized what was going to happen! If I had only asked some of my friends in the States to loan me a little bit of money to invest. If I could just have another chance, knowing what I know now!* But it's too late. The opportunity is gone. I know of one mission group that had simply bargained for a long-term lease on a piece of real estate in Tokyo, and when the boom hit, that group was given one million dollars cash just to break the lease. But that is nothing compared to the loss many of us are going to feel when we suddenly appear before our Lord—when we suddenly awaken to the realization that we had our opportunity to make the right kind of investments but failed to do so. Suddenly it will become clear why Jesus said, "Not on earth, but in heaven. Not where thieves and rust and moths can get it, but where it will pay dividends for eternity.

There are those who have already tuned me out, and others are simply reading all of this without much comprehension. I am sure that there are some who are saying, "But what should we do? What is it that Jesus is saying to us in this command?" First of all, we need to see where He is putting the emphasis. I believe the key is in the expression, "Lay not up *for yourselves*." In the parable of the rich fool, Jesus says, "So is he that layeth up treasure *for himself*, and is not rich toward God" (Luke 12:21, italics added). What is your motive in business? What is your motive in building your bank account, in accumulating material goods? Is it all for yourself (of course, 10 per-

cent is for the Lord!), or is it for God? The Scriptures
certainly teach that there are those within Christ's body
who have the gift of giving, and we can safely assume that
one with this gift must have some good means of getting
in order to be able to give. This person may have to be
involved in investing huge sums of money in order to
make money to carry out his ministry of giving. His
ministry, therefore, might possibly require a style of living far above that which those of us without that gift find
ourselves accustomed to. That brother may need a plane,
while I can get along quite well with a bicycle. It is not
that we can measure our dedication to the Lord by what
we do without or by what we do not have. Unfortunately,
I have met some missionaries who seem to feel that they
are more spiritual because they do without certain things.
No, it is not that at all. The question is, is it for ourselves,
or is it for God?

Is that new and larger house for yourself, or is it for
God? Is it going to bring glory to Him, or is it simply to
make you feel a bit closer to the Joneses? For years our
missionaries on the mission field of northern Japan lived
in typical (in those days) Japanese houses with sliding
paper doors. Sometimes those paper doors were all there
was between them and the cold, blowing snow outside,
and even when the doors were made of wood and glass
they were made to allow free passage of the winds. But
that was all the housing there was for a time and many
accepted it as from the Lord, thankful for even that much.
The time came, however, when building supplies became
more plentiful, We built better houses, and, naturally, better houses cost more money. A few more years passed and
it became possible to purchase insulation for our houses.
Today when our mission builds a new missionary home it
is assumed from the start that we will put in central heat-

ing. Now, would it not be more spiritual to forego the
insulation, the subflooring, the furnace, and use that
money for "the Lord's work"? Well, to put it in the words
of one missionary wife, "I don't really think the chill
blains I used to have every winter made me any more
spiritual, and I know they kept me from being as efficient
as I might have been." No, we believe that comfortable
housing makes us more effective in our work, not to mention what the Japanese might think if we were to continue
to live in a fashion they gave up years ago! But at the same
time, the missionary has learned to be comfortable in a
smaller house because of the extreme cost of building in
Japan today. On what basis would you expect the missionary field conference to determine housing policies?
Should missionaries adjust their standard of living to that
of the people in their supporting churches back in the
homeland? Should they build for themselves? Or is it
possible that there is such a thing as building a house for
God? Unfortunately, the missionaries are human and they
do make mistakes, lots of them! But by and large the missionaries I have worked with have sought to please the
Lord even in the matter of building missionary homes. To
do this, many factors had to be considered. There is the
matter of the local culture and the missionary's testimony
in the community. Should the missionary follow the local
patterns? And, if so, to what degree? Until recently the
Japanese house builder was not the least bit concerned
about building a warm house and considered the expense
of insulation beyond its worth. But because of his great
love for nature he would spend vast sums to have one or
two large boulders and a couple of big trees hauled in to
complete his little garden. And those gardens are beautiful! But somehow or other the missionary found that he
could enjoy his garden better, even if he had to start with

a few seedlings and wait for them to grow big and tall, if he spent less on the garden and included insulation in the walls of his house. He felt that the health and general well-being of his family enabled him to do a better job for the Lord. Granted, it would take a few years for his trees to gain the height of his neighbor's, but once the construction of the house was completed, the insulation did not show and his house looked just like most of the others in the neighborhood. The problem for the missionary in a poorer country will of course be more difficult than for the missionary in Japan, since minimum living standards for the American are far above maximum standards for many parts of the world, but even so, the basic factor must be—for self, or for God?

Again I ask, what are your guidelines for your everyday financial dealings and decisions? Do you have eternity's values in view or are you geared to the standards of this world? Are you giving any thought to eternal investments? If you are not, then you will find this entire chapter rather hard to follow. But if you are concerned about eternal investments, then your living standards, your expense accounts, and your bank statements will all be affected. In spite of the fact that this kind of teaching and preaching is not popular, I believe it is time that we evangelicals quit kidding ourselves about finances.

Some of you may be interested in what is behind the writing of this particular chapter. I am a member of a fellowship of Bible-believing people who have been known for their interest in and concern for world missions. In fact, our fellowship came into being as a missionary organization. Missionaries sent out under our organization must deputate among local churches in the homeland and wait on the Lord to lead some of those churches to underwrite their annual support before they can leave for the mission field. The Lord has greatly blessed this policy, and today there are over five hundred missionaries serving Jesus Christ around the world under the sponsorship of our foreign mission, in spite of the fact that local churches in this organization number only around twelve hundred, many of them small churches. Over the years I have heard a great deal of concern expressed by some who feel that our few churches are reaching what they call the "saturation point." That is, we will soon be supporting the maximum possible number of missionaries, and if we do not start more churches in the homeland, we will have to start curtailing our missionary outreach. This is an illustration of how we are kidding ourselves about finances. Those who are sounding the alarm are not blind. They are seriously facing a definite problem, but they are facing it with an incorrect assumption. The problem they see is that finances are not forthcoming in sufficient quantity to meet the opportunities our missionaries around the world are facing. It is sometimes requiring up to two years of deputation for a missionary candidate to secure his support. Again, referring to Japan, the cost of supporting a missionary in that land today as compared with support twenty-five years ago has risen by over 400 percent. Housing for one family, if new construction is necessary, will cost anywhere from $60,000 up, depending on where that missionary is to be placed. Our missionaries and Japanese leaders in Japan have drawn up a twenty-year goal of seeing 100 churches planted in the major cities of northern Japan by 1995, and they have sent out a plea for more workers, both foreign and national. God is answering those prayers and new missionary recruits are coming forward. But where is the money going to come from? Remember the saturation point. We are almost giving the maximum we can afford. Do you believe that? If you do, then you, too, are kidding yourself.

Do we need new churches in the homeland? We certainly do. Should we be concerned about starting new churches in the homeland? We certainly should. Does our worldwide missionary outreach really depend on the establishing of new churches in the homeland? Very possibly it does—if we continue the status quo. If we satisfy ourselves by continuing to think and act as we have been acting, then we must have more people giving a small portion of what they have in order to have more for getting the gospel out. But if we are willing to get back to the Scriptures and reevaluate what we are doing, if we are willing to put those scriptural principles to work, if we are willing to quit kidding ourselves about finances— then we will discover that there is no such thing as a saturation point in the economy of God. Yes, from man's standpoint there was no possible way the widow's pot of oil could contain enough to fill all the jars and jugs her sons borrowed from the neighbors, but it did. There was no possible way that little fellow's lunch could meet the need of five thousand hungry people, but it did. There was no way Moses could provide for the people out there in the wilderness, but they ate three squares per day. And when the people of God today apply the principles of God from the Word of God, they too can have the provision of God. Saturation point? Maybe your God is that small— mine isn't.

We spoke of the small fellowship to which I belong. A friend of mine ministers among our churches by assisting individuals in setting up wills and annuity programs. He has publicly stated that from what little knowledge he has of the financial resources of those with whom he works, and they are basically those within our particular fellowship of churches, he knows of 5 billion dollars that is essentially not being touched for the Lord's work. When I questioned him about the figure, he replied, "Jim, I said 5 billion publicly, but I honestly believe it is closer to 15 billion."

Now if you ask me if the people known as Conservative Baptists believe the Word of God, I will reply with a hearty, "They certainly do!" And if you ask me if they believe what the Word of God has to say about material possessions, I will again reply in the affirmative. But if you ask me if their practices and financial policies show forth such belief, I will try to change the subject, for that "saturation point" talk still rings in my ears and sticks in my throat.

Lest I leave some wrong impressions, let me go on to say that there are those within my own fellowship of churches who give and who give generously. My long missionary experience has brought me in touch with some dear saints of God who have even given sacrificially. And I am confident that this is also true of other groups of evangelical believers. However, the fact remains that the evangelical church in America in general and most believers in particular are kidding themselves about finances when it comes to their missionary outreach.

It is my conviction that the God we serve is the God of Elijah, Elisha, and Moses. He was able to keep the widow's jar of oil flowing until the needs were met. When Elijah asked the widow of Zarephath for a morsel of bread, she responded generously, even though she thought she had only enough for one last meal for her son and herself. The man of God had said, "First, provide for me. I am God's representative. Then prepare for yourself and your son. Your supplies will last until the famine is over." "Seek ye first the kingdom of God" is how the Lord stated the same principle years later. Yes, the God we serve is still ready, willing, and anxious to keep some oil flowing if He can find men with whom He can trust the oil.

I recall hearing some years ago one of the Hillis brothers relate the story of a European farmer who came to America and purchased a farm in the Midwest. He knew no English, and a neighboring farmer who was a Christian went over in the evenings after chores were finished and started teaching his new friend English conversation. Before long, the man from Europe not only learned to speak English, he also came to a personal knowledge of the Lord Jesus Christ. The soul-winner did a good job of discipling, for when the man accepted Jesus Christ as Savior he also owned Him as Lord. The new believer told the Lord that from that point in time on he was going to start farming for Jesus. As I recall the story, his prayer went something like this, "Lord, You have saved me and You have purchased me. Thus, I belong to You. From now on I am going to work for You. To care for my family properly I will need about $400 per month. Everything else that You send in is Yours."

That farmer kept his promise to the Lord and for a number of years went on farming. Some years were good ones and he had a good bit to give to the Lord's work. Other times were not so good, and he just barely made enough to keep his family. One day oil was found on that farm, and overnight the farmer's income jumped way up. His lawyer came to him and suggested that he and his family move into town and that he play the part of the prosperous businessman he now was. The oil rigs on the farm made farming impossible. But the farmer wasn't interested in his lawyer's suggestions. He had been farming for Jesus Christ, and he decided that he would continue to do just that. Staying on the $400 monthly salary and giving the proceeds from the oil wells to the Lord's work, the farmer moved farther west, purchased yet another farm, and went right on farming for Jesus Christ.

That story thrilled me, and I started telling it in every church I visited on deputation. But let me tell you about a fear many preachers have when they are telling second-hand stories. We are always a little concerned that our version of the story might not be just exactly how the events really took place. Maybe the story was dressed up a bit for the purpose of making it a better illustration — and maybe I will get caught telling it to someone who knows the facts in the case. Well, that is exactly what happened to me. I was telling this story in a little rural church in eastern Colorado one evening when I noticed several persons in the audience actively paying attention. Soon there were several smiles and two or three heads started nodding as I continued the story. They had heard it before! Now I would find out if the details were correct.

Sure enough, after the message was over and the service dismissed, several people came right up to me at the front of the church building, and one of them asked, "Was your story about Mr. So and So?"

"Yes, it was," I replied, "but how did you know his name?" (I had not given his name as I related the story.)

"Oh, we know the story very well. You see, his widow lives down the road a little. When they struck oil on their first farm, they moved on out here to eastern Colorado, bought a wheat farm, and went right on farming, just as you said."

"Well," I asked, "did it all happen just the way I told the story?"

"Yes, it did. But why didn't you finish telling the whole story?"

"Finish telling it? I did finish. I told all that I knew about the family."

"But you didn't tell the most fantastic part. They moved out here and started farming again, and they farmed here for quite some time. Several years ago the husband was killed by a logging truck in an accident in northern California, but before he died they struck oil on his wheat ranch here in Colorado! His widow is still writing checks for missions all around the world!

How many oil wells do you own? You say that you don't have any? Not even one? Could it be that perhaps the Lord could not trust you with one? (I don't have any either!) The Lord is not short of oil wells. The problem is that He is short of those to whom He can entrust them.

Don't you see it? Here is a local church that wants to take on the support of a new missionary couple, but the church's budget is fully pledged now. The people want to stand behind this couple, who happen to be members of that church, but the couple lack $10,000 a year in support. No, that isn't their salary only. It includes salary, transportation to and from the field, language study, evangelism work, funds for the field, children's schooling, and many other items, but it is all necessary and must be underwritten before they may leave for their field. Under normal circumstances—the status quo I referred to earlier—the Lord will have to increase the incomes of the people in that congregation by $100,000 before they will feel free to underwrite the needed support, but in no way do the people in that church need such an increase in their incomes. Nevertheless, the Lord wants that missionary couple out, so He blesses the business of several of the members to the point where total income of four families increases by $135,000. Wonderful! They have avoided the "saturation point." The missionaries will get their underwriting. But it does not work that way. You see, when the four families have their incomes increased, two of them feel that their houses are really just too small; the members of one family decide that since the Lord has blessed their family so much, they need a swimming pool in the backyard so they can entertain the church youth group once in a while; and the folk in the fourth family find that they can now afford a new boat. Of course, Sunday is the only time they can really get out to enjoy it. To top things off, the church offerings do go up a bit, for the pastor is a very wise pastor, and he is careful to compliment the two families on their beautiful new homes and to tell the entire church about the generosity of the family that now has swimming parties for the church youth (once a quarter—the rest of the time it serves three members of the family occasionally). And he tactfully keeps after the boating family so that even when they do not make it to church they do get their offerings in. But when the church offerings go up, somebody notices the surplus and remembers the need for a new computer in the church office to help keep track of the church finances. So by the time the missions committee gets around to its recommendation to the church, about all it can recommend is that the church pray harder for its missionaries and maybe another church can help with their support.

Sarcasm? Perhaps, but if truth is stranger than fiction, it is also stranger than sarcasm. What you have just read is happening in various degrees in our churches across our land, and it is just another reason why the laborers are still few.

How about you? Would you be interested in going to work for the Lord? Would you be interested in giving the Lord an opportunity to trust you with an oil well, or a gold mine? Well, just show Him that you can be trusted with the paper route you now have and maybe you will graduate to the oil fields. Why not give the Lord a figure for your own personal and family needs and promise Him everything above? And if you feel before the Lord that you could honor Him with a swimming pool or a new house or a boat, tell Him about it. Generally, if the Lord can trust a man with an oil well, He can also trust him with a boat.

Jesus Christ wants you in the investment business. He wants you to invest in His business of getting the Word out to a lost and dying world; He wants you to invest in His business of building His church worldwide.

What would happen if a few hundred of His people quit kidding themselves about finances and gave Him an opportunity to open the jars of oil? What would happen if some local churches would do likewise, giving God a ceiling on their own operational expenses and promising all over and above for getting the message out to the regions beyond? Let's quit kidding ourselves and find out.

But there is more that needs to be said about finances, because our responsibility does not end when the dollar lands in the offering plate. Stewardship has to do with our giving, but it also has to do with how that which we have given is used. Here again, many of the Lord's people have been fooling themselves concerning finances. Too many people, as a result of their emotions, never have a question about the way their gifts will be administered. After all, that missionary speaker gave a powerful message. He told us about his work, and he is doing such a fine piece of work! Why, I don't have to worry about what he does with my money. He couldn't do anything wrong. I must tell you that the Kingdom has not arrived yet. Missionaries are people, just like you. Have you ever made mistakes? Did you ever show bad judgment? Have you ever been saved from a serious error because someone was overseeing your work or because you had to submit a report? It happens to missionaries all the time. I am not saying that missionaries in general are dishonest. They are not. Missionaries are generally dedicated people who desperately want to do that which is right, but because they are people, they are sometimes wrong. Sincere, but sincerely wrong! For the most part, missionaries are trained in theology, not business. I have known some missionaries who have little concept of how to handle money. They are strong in faith and they can trust the Lord to send in vast amounts of that green stuff, but it almost seems that the more that comes in, the less care they use in spending it—and that is true of some organizations as well. As a steward of Jesus Christ, you need to know how and where your gifts are being used, and you need to be sure that that "wonderful missionary work in the regions beyond" is being properly supervised. After all, that tremendous speaker who touched your heart and pocketbook probably touched hundreds of others in other churches, and quite possibly he is receiving far more than he really needs for his own ministry, while others, because they are not powerful missionary speakers, might be in need.

Perhaps you are asking, "Well, isn't the Lord able to care for the needs of all His workers?" Yes, He certainly is, and He has instructed us to do all things decently and in order. He established a church and a form of government for that church. He gave instruction for the selection of officers for the local body, and if we follow His instructions there will be proper supervision and the needs of all will be met. This, unfortunately, is not what is happening when God's people give outside their local church channels or outside reputable mission organizations. As stated earlier in this book, there are no doubt some independent missionaries who, although they have no overseeing group over them and do not have to give any detailed accounting of the finances entrusted to them, are perfectly honest in every detail and completely businesslike in their dealings. But the dangers involved are legion and I have seen enough on just one mission field to convince me that I could never approve of supporting an independent missionary unless there were some special precautions taken. In the first place, the body-truth concept of Scripture does not seem to provide for one member of the body running off doing his own thing. The church is to work as a complete unit. We have yet to see or hear of a foot or a hand which is not able to get along with other members of the body and thus pulls itself loose from the body to run off and go its own way while at the same time expecting the body to supply its needs. But that is exactly what is happening in the church today.

Now before I get myself too far out on a limb, let me make it clear that I am writing from personal experience, and my experiences have been limited to just one field. Even then I would not profess to have the total picture of that one entire field. However, twenty-five years of limited experience on just a portion of one mission field causes me to ask some pointed questions. Why work independently? Was it too difficult getting along with other missionaries? Was it too difficult having to give and take? Were the mission's financial policies too restrictive? Did close supervision over work and financial policies present a problem? Did being a member of a team make it difficult to paint for the supporting churches at home a picture that was a bit overrealistic? I intend to develop this a bit further in the next chapter, but this matter definitely needs to be considered when we are thinking about finances. Just exactly what are you and your church doing with the Lord's money?

In chapter two I told you about an independent missionary who received money from his supporting churches in the States with which to build a church building, and he really did intend to build it. I saw the blueprints for the church building. But before he could get the building up, he passed away. The land on which he was going to build and the large house on that land passed to his adopted daughter and then, when she died, to her daughter. I know of another case in which God's people in the States provided for a lovely piece of property for missionary living quarters and a church meeting place, but the missionary involved was not related to any mission organization, and that property, today worth many thousands of dollars, is no longer related in any way to the Lord's work. If the the Lord asked for an accounting of the one, five, and ten talents, is it not possible that He may someday ask us how we used that which He entrusted to us? We had better quit kidding ourselves about finances.

There is yet another principle the Lord gave to us in the so-called Sermon on the Mount. In Matthew 6:2 He said:

> Therefore when thou doest thine alms, do not sound a trumpet before thee, as the hypocrites do in the synagogues and in the streets, that they may have glory of men. Verily I say unto you, They have their reward.

Why do you give? How do you give? Do you give for reward? Do you expect to receive something in return? Well, you certainly should be giving for reward, for the Lord Himself told us to do so. Time and time again He tells us how to do things so that the Father in heaven will be pleased to reward us. In 2 John 8 the apostle admonishes us to work for a full reward, so if you feel that it is more spiritual not to think about rewards, you must be some kind of super saint. I want all the rewards the Lord has provided for me! But the Lord says that there is a possibility of getting rewards here and now, and from the sound of Matthew 6:2, such rewards are not worth much. Those about whom Jesus was speaking gave in order to earn the reward of men's praise—and they got it. That was it, full and final. It is my conviction that many of God's people today are getting exactly the same kind of rewards for their giving.

Take for example the well-to-do Christian businessman who leaves a large sum in his will for some sort of a memorial at a Christian school or even out on the mission field. Is he thereby laying up treasure in heaven? Well, I am not going to be dogmatic about it, for I cannot see the heart as God sees it, but somehow a disturbing question keeps popping up in the back of my mind. While that brother was still alive, the money was his to transfer to his account in heaven, but after death, does he get credit for it? He will get the praise of men for that memorial, but is he still really interested in that reward? I doubt it. It seems to me that the Lord is far more concerned about the attitude of the giver's heart than He is about the amount of the gift, and the Scriptures seem to say that the giving that really counts is the giving that is done strictly out of love and without any desire for recognition from man. That is the giving that becomes an eternal investment.

Would it not be wise for all of us to check the Scripture to see if our investments are really eternal in nature or if we have been getting most of the rewards here and now? With eternity's values in view, let's quit kidding ourselves about finances.

6

Let's Quit Kidding Ourselves About The Missionary

There are several areas about which it is very easy for the general public in our churches to be, putting it tactfully, misinformed about missionaries, and often this is definitely in spite of all the missionary himself has said or written. In recent years we have all read or heard stories about the funny impressions many people have of missionaries. In fact, almost every missionary conference I attend will have some spot on the program for some humor, and inevitably the spotlight focuses on the out-of-style clothing or old-fashioned hairdo of the missionary. In fact, so much attention has been given to these aspects that most missionaries today are probably more fashion conscious than the average church member, and, as a result, they probably are tempted to spend more on clothing and hairstyles than their incomes can afford. In a country such as Japan today, the missionary generally dresses in styles and fashions much the same as those in the United States, so this is not such a drastic problem for him. The missionary from some of the third world countries, however, will still find that when he returns to his native land he has again fallen behind, for example, in styles and fashions. His unawareness of this, or his seeming unconcern, should make it evident to the thinking Christian that the missionary has been taken up with more important things—things related to eternity. He has been involved with the souls of men, seeking to translate the Scriptures into their language, seeking to turn men and women with little or no clothing to the One who can clothe them with robes of righteousness, and somehow the latest fashion notes from Paris have escaped his attention. But do not be too harsh to the missionary home on furlough, for before he is in the home church very long he will awaken to the importance of "getting in style." His values will soon be readjusted, and, if he is given an even chance, it will soon be difficult to tell which one is the missionary. Perhaps that is the way it should be—or should it?

Because the missionary comes home wearing the same suit he had when he left for the field, some suppose that he could not afford a new one, while others assume he has failed to keep abreast of the latest in fashions. Some react with sympathy, others with contempt, and both are guilty of kidding themselves about the missionary.

Then there are those within our churches who constantly write to the missionary, telling him how much they appreciate his sacrificial spirit. "How wonderful that you are willing to leave *everything* and go away to a foreign land and suffer so for Jesus!" On the other hand, there are those in the same church who just know that the missionary could never get that kind of salary "if he had to come home and work for a living!" And here again we have people kidding themselves about missionaries.

My wife and I have often said that if we had our lives to live over again, we would choose to "leave all" anytime when we could have the opportunity of raising our family in a foreign land where they could have the advantages of experiencing a different culture, learning a second language, and sharing in the thrill of seeing people come under the sound of the gospel for the first time. If you really believe that the missionary "leaves all" when he goes out to serve the Lord in a distant part of the world, you are indeed kidding yourself about the missionary.

Yes, it is true that the missionary does leave his homeland and his parents. He must leave certain aspects of his culture, his home church, his home town, but this business of "leaving all" is a misnomer to say the least. It has been our experience that we gained far more than we left. In the first place, besides the advantages of living and learning in a different culture, as mentioned above, just in the preparation for going overseas we gained a host of committed friends—co-workers, or prayer partners, as they are called—that we might never have had otherwise. We have broken out of the 6 percent vision to the point where we at least have gained a little experience about some of the other 94 percent. We have had the experience of being able to rethink some of the scriptural teachings in the Word while living in an admitted non-Christian environment, and, at the same time, we have never lacked for anything. But more than this, we have had the utmost thrill that we believe can come to anyone. We have had the joy of hearing a dying woman whisper, "Thank you for coming. If you had not come, I never would have known about Jesus. I am going to meet Him now!" "Leave everything?" Don't you believe it! Granted, the missionary salary may leave something to be desired from the economic standpoint, but the earned income is out of this world!

Much of the erroneous thinking pertaining to missionaries is the fault of the missionary himself, but, on the other hand, much of it is in spite of all the missionary can say or do. The fact remains, if the average Christian in the average local church would take the time to get some factual information about the missionary, we could stop kidding ourselves, and if we stop kidding ourselves about the missionary, we will find ourselves in a position from which we can help do something about the shortage of laborers.

Just exactly what kind of critter is this missionary? I remember one of our missionary ladies who, while on furlough some years ago, was visiting in a home on Sunday. While the mother was busy getting dinner ready, she suggested that the missionary lady just relax in the living room and play with the little girl in the home. Out came the dolls and dresses, and the little girl and the missionary lady played for quite some time. All of a sudden, however, the little girl jumped up and ran into the kitchen. My friend overheard the little girl say to her mother, "Mommy, she's just like one of us!" Now perhaps you smile at that, but that little girl got an insight into the missionary that many far more mature Christians still lack. The missionary is just like us! Just exactly like us! Flesh and bones and hands and feet, likes and dislikes, feelings, and reactions, emotions, prejudices, opinions, hunger, desires, and so on. He was born just as you were—in sin—and he was sought after by the same Savior who sought after you. Yes, believe it or not, that missionary has the same sinful nature you have and thus the same temptations, the same frustrations, the same battles, the same desperate need to use 1 John 1:9 continually. When a young person completes his schooling and finally stands before the group that commissions missionaries for the missionary task, he may receive a new assignment, a new title, a new passport and eventually a new language—but the old nature still remains. Now I know that many of you are saying, "Woll, so what ? We know all that. You haven't told us anything new."

But do you really know it? Are you sure that you have not been kidding yourself about the missionary? Don't you really believe that the missionary is different? Don't you really believe that he is somehow endowed with a bit more holy nature than you or the average Christian in your church? Come on now, be honest with me! Listen, if you hear that a certain missionary couple on the field is having marital problems, wouldn't that shock you? If you heard that a mission board had to drop a missionary because of outright dishonesty on the part of that missionary, wouldn't you be a bit surprised? If word got to you that drugs, smoking, and drinking were problems with which the board of directors of a certain missionary-children's school had to deal, wouldn't it cause you to raise your eyebrows just a little? If you heard about a shotgun wedding for two missionary children, would that simply slip by you as just another indication of the moral decay of our day and age? Well, to adapt an expression frequently heard on radio and T.V., "The stories you have just heard are true –only the names have been changed to protect the guilty." Does this surprise you? Then you have been kidding yourself about the missionary.

Now before you put this book down and rush to the telephone, let me hasten to add that these things are not the norm among missionaries anymore than they are the norm in your local church. In fact, what I am saying is that the missionary is simply the extension of your local church overseas, and what can and does happen to those left at home can and possibly will happen among your missionaries overseas. If you do not realize this, you are not being the co-laborer your missionary wants and needs. If you do not fully understand this basic fact, you are going to help the enemy set that missionary up for a terrific fall. That missionary needs your constant prayer support, for in some ways he is going to face far more difficult temptations out there than you face at home. That missionary needs the restraining influences of fellow missionaries and mission boards to help him guard against the same natural tendencies you might face in the business or social world here at home. Would you deposit your money in a bank that has no governing rules or regulations, no audits, and no reporting mechanisms—even if all the bank workers were born-again Christians? Are you willing to give your offerings to a local church where the pastor runs the entire show, handles all the money, and makes no reports to anybody? Even if he is a fine preacher? Even if he has two earned Ph.Ds? Well, then how can you handle your missionary giving in that way? You can, but only if you have been kidding yourself about the missionary and his frailties.

May I use a personal illustration? Years ago when we started a new camp ministry in northern Japan, I found myself having to handle the finances for the project. Actually, I had what I considered to be a foolproof method of accounting. I had one large sheet of paper with two columns, an income column and an outgo column. I could subtract the smaller from the larger at any time and know just exactly where I was financially. This presented no problem whatsoever with the budget, simply because we did not have a budget! There was no need, in the very early stages of our camp ministry, to differentiate between building money and camp-store money, or equipment money and salaries. There was no such need for two reasons. First, we did not have a building, or a store, or equipment, or hired workers, and, second, we did not have that kind of money. But the Lord gave us a vision for a year-round ministry with real estate, buildings, equipment, and paid staff, and little by little He began to send in the necessary finances. All of a sudden I found that my two columns were getting longer and longer. I could still balance them and still tell quite quickly if I were in the red or the black, but for some reason one of my missionary co-workers, who happened to be our field treasurer, began to give me the impression that he was not sold on my method of bookkeeping. The fact that he had worked in a bank possibly had something to do with his thinking, I don't know, but he kept telling me about credits and debits and balance sheets, and before long he had me so confused that I didn't know what to do. We were just starting to handle money into the thousands of dollars and, quite frankly, I did not know how to do it properly. Then, in an unguarded moment my dear wife let it slip that she had taken bookkeeping in school, and she seemed to understand all the talk about credits and debits and stuff. Well, guess who became the bookkeeper? The point is that as a missionary I was doing the best I could. I was trying to be strictly honest, but sincerity and honesty were not sufficient. We were handling thousands of dollars of the Lord's money and our relationship to an organization required us to follow accepted methods of good stewardship.

But another area about which we can fool ourselves is that of the missionary's responsibilities. The modern missionary, even the one serving in the third world countries, is facing responsibilities often far different from those the missionary of thirty, forty, or fifty years ago faced. If he is not engaged in training leadership in the local national church, he is engaged in working with the leadership that is already present, and this means that he needs the very best in training and preparation. In one sense I doubt that this is any different from the way it was in the days of the early church, for it is clear in the Scriptures that when the Holy Spirit told the church to set aside some men for some missionary endeavors, He chose the best men the church had. If the church today feels that anything less than the best will do in our day, we are still guilty of kidding ourselves about the missionary. If ever the missionary challenge facing the church demanded the best the church could give in the way of workers, that demand should be seen and recognized today. Missions need men and women who are capable of adjusting to a new and different culture, men and women who are keen enough to face the challenge of putting an unknown language into writing, men and women who are keen enough to train leadership for churches in highly educated countries. The mission field demands and must have the very best. I know of missionaries who washed out on the mission field and returned to the States to have a very successful pastoral ministry, but I have yet to meet the man who washed out as a pastor in the homeland but proved to be successful on the mission field.

Now I hardly expect to encounter any vocal opposition on this point, even among those at home who are not basically interested in missions. But I have been very much aware for years of those who are definitely kidding themselves about the missionary at this very point—and this type of thinking is to be found at all levels of our Christian society. Missions? Great. We are all for missions. Why we even have a missionary barrel in our church, and we keep it filled with things for the missionary. The missionary deserves the best—the best old coats and dresses we have. Why, some people are even willing to spend hours sewing up those old clothes so the missionary can use them. You have no doubt heard the story of the lady who took the time and effort to dry out two dozen tea bags to send to a missionary in India. Now that dear lady, I am sure, would not put forth that kind of time and effort for just anybody, but she did for the missionary. And in the box she enclosed a letter in which she explained that the tea bags had been used only once and were still good for two or three more cups of tea each. The fact that she herself had got the best cup of tea out of each bag first never seemed to register. She was for missions and the missionary! Missions were first—after herself. Perhaps you are asking, "Well, would it have been better had she not sent any tea bags at all?" No, I am sure that the missionary who received the package would appreciate the effort and the love expressed. And if tea were hard to come by in India, the missionary would also appreciate even the secondhand tea bags, but that is not the point. The point is that in too many cases the average Christian has been fooled into believing that when it comes to missions, anything will do—our leftovers, our castouts, our pennies (after all the needs and wants have been met in the home church first!).

Have you ever heard the comment, "With all his abilities and talents—what a shame to waste all that out on the mission field"? Perhaps you have never said it, but have you ever thought it? Years ago I knew of a promising young fellow who was interested in the possibility of serving the Lord overseas. He was a gifted teacher and his services were desired by a fine evangelical seminary in the States. Now I do not pretend to know what the Lord desired in the way of service from that young man, but I shall never forget the feeling I had when the statement was made that his abilities and talents could be so much more effective at home. That particular story came to mind again just recently when I read this statement by Michael C. Griffiths in *Give Up Your Small Ambitions* (Chicago: Moody, 1970):

> One of the tragedies of evangelical missionary work has been that so often they have been satisfied with lower-level Bible schools instead of crowning these by providing theological teaching on the highest level. One reason has been the lack of sufficiently well-qualified missionaries. Out of some 1,500 evangelical missionaries in Japan recently, not one could be found who was competent enough in both languages to check a new Japanese translation against the original Hebrew. Liberals and Roman Catholics could have done it, but not Evangelicals. *This suggests that a certain number of the finest theological brains ought to be prepared to give their services overseas* [p. 47, italics added].

Again I quote the same author:

> If it takes a good mind to lecture in theology at home, it takes a better one elsewhere in another language and another culture [p. 47].

Griffiths served for some years on the field in Japan, and I am sure he is writing from that background when he refers to lower-level Bible schools instead of theological teaching on the highest level. This very problem has plagued the church-planting efforts of my own mission group in Japan for years, and we are still not over the top. I cannot help but feel that part of the reason for this is that some are still kidding themselves about the importance of sending the very best.

But, again, lest there be a misunderstanding, let me hasten to add that I do not necessarily feel that the best always means seminary-level training. Certainly it would seem to mean that, and possibly more, when we are thinking of professional teachers for the mission field. We cannot train seminary teachers in Japan with men who only have college degrees, that is obvious. But just as some seminary professors would never be able to function effectively in a pastorate, so some seminary graduates could never make it through the first term on a foreign mission field. When I speak of the best, I am not limiting that to scholastic training, important as that may be. Some missionary projects might prove to be far more successful with fewer scholars and more workers who have first proved themselves in the homeland. For instance, in a church-planting ministry on a foreign field it is very possible that the degreeless missionary who had started one or two churches in his own country would be far more effective than the seminary graduate who has yet to get his feet wet in church planting. The successful missionary who lacks scholastic training will in most cases seek opportunities to further his training either during furlough or by organized personal study, but when I speak of the best, I am referring to the quality of the worker and not necessarily to his polishing.

I could wish that mission boards and churches would give more consideration to the actual experience the missionary candidate has had and, if necessary, let up a bit on the scholastic requirements. As stated earlier, a scholastic deficiency can always be made up during a furlough after the young missionary has learned from experience where his deficiencies are, but sending out the inexperienced is, in effect, gambling with the Lord's money. Does it not seem a bit strange that many churches in the homeland refuse to consider a prospective pastor who has not had a number of years of experience, yet, at the same time, they will send a young seminary graduate with no experience whatsoever off to a foreign land to face the challenge of a new language, a new culture, and, quite possibly, a church-planting ministry in an area far greater in size and population than that of the home church? To me it is yet another proof that we are still kidding ourselves about the missionary, about his task, and about our responsibility to them both.

Still another area of concern is the failure of the church at home to face up to the missionary and his opportunities. Never before in the history of the Christian church have the opportunities been greater. While the enemy and his forces are talking of moritoriums on sending missionaries and some people seem to be mesmerized by the closed doors, the fact remains that the laborers are few. There simply are not enough workers, not enough senders, not enough finances even to begin to realize the opportunities the church of Jesus Christ has around the world today. This in no way should be construed as meaning that Jesus is failing or even that He is falling behind in His program. As I tried to point out in an earlier chapter, Jesus said He was going to do the building, and that is exactly what He is doing. But He is still looking for men and women who want to get in on the action, men and women who want to do some heavy investing in eternal stocks and bonds, and He has lots of job opportunities for all interested parties. The church of Jesus Christ has been assigned a task by her Commander in Chief, and the church is not putting full effort into that task. We are guilty of partial obedience at best. God so loved the world that He gave His own Son—and He desires that the entire world know about it. We are told in the Word that our enemy is cunning, that he is a deceiver; and he has been deceiving the church of Jesus Christ in our day and age as never before. We are instructed in the Word to "love not the world, neither the things that are in the world" (1 John 2:15), but vast numbers of God's people are basically motivated by love for things of the world. Granted, some of those "things" may even be good things—things like beautiful church buildings, Christian organizations, and church-related programs. But even these, when they divert us from the number one task assigned by our Commander, are no better than the "things" people of the world seek after.

What is there in the life and program of the average evangelical church today which gives any indication that we do not belong to this world's system? What is there about your church which speaks to the fact that we are pilgrims and strangers here? It is my conviction that the same materialistic philosophy that motivates the secular world is very much alive and well in the church of Jesus Christ today, and the tragedy is that many within the church are not even aware of it. Some preachers who can hold forth from their pulpits against greed and covetousness, doing a masterful job of exegeting the scriptural passages dealing with the subject, are themselves manifesting those very qualities as they strive for bigger congregations, larger church buildings, greater places of importance, bigger followings, I can almost hear the apostle Paul saying:

> Therefore thou art inexcusable, O man, whosoever thou art that judgest: for wherein thou judgest another, thou condemnest thyself; for thou that judgest doest the same things [Rom. 2:1].

When I was a young boy in Tucson we had a number of smaller churches in our town that had been started under the ministry of our pastor. One of those churches was pastored by a godly man who worked with the church until it grew fairly large, and then he left. I did not know at the time where he went, but years later I renewed contact with him and have followed his ministry with interest ever since. His was a unique ministry in that he always seemed to accept calls from smaller, struggling churches whenever he felt a change was in order. How strange. In a day when God almost always "leads" to bigger and bigger pastorates, how strange that this fellow went the other way. No, it isn't a bit strange, for this brother was motivated by a simple desire to serve His Lord. He had no ambition for bigger and better things for himself, just a burning desire to serve the Lord and a burden for lost souls. He did not push a missionary program in his churches, his entire life and ministry was a missionary program, and that is just as it should be.

> And ye shall be witnesses unto me *both* in Jerusalem, and in all Judaea, and in Samaria, and unto the uttermost part of the earth [Acts 1:8, italics added].

As a result I look upon this brother as being one of the more "well-to-do" among us. He may be living on his social security funds presently, but he really has it laid away in heaven. He must have most of his rewards still coming, for he hasn't received too many of them down here. He didn't even get an honorary degree from any school, but I am rather confident that the Lord has a different system of giving honorary degrees—and a different reason for giving them.

Before you come to some conclusions of your own, let me confess something. I have been involved in missions for twenty-five years, and I am prejudiced. I am prejudiced to the point where I believe that churches that have a missionary program are simply not true New Tes-

tament churches. The New Testament church did not
have a missionary program. She *was* a missionary program. She existed for one primary purpose, and that was
to be a witness to the world—the entire world. The New
Testament church felt out of place in her world and was
eager for her Lord to come and get her. In her eagerness
she was busy—busy getting the message out by every
means possible. Certainly she did not neglect those in
need of her message right there in Jerusalem, but the
basic thrust of the one book in the Bible which gives us
the history of that early church is that of how she reached
out into the then-known world to spread the good news.
And any thinking person who reads that early record of
the church cannot help but notice the dissimilarities between then and now. Somehow the drive-in church service doesn't seem to fit the picture. And neither do a lot of
other things that are more popular in evangelical
churches than drive-in services. But first and foremost we
must confess that the most glaring difference is in the
area of dedication to the task assigned to the church by
her Master. Whereas the primary ministry of that early
church was to reach ever farther out to a lost and dying
world with the message of life and light, our primary
ministry today has been to "hold the fort." Yes, now and
then we send out little squads to do some probing here
and there. We go to a bit of expense to equip a few fellow
soldiers and send them out to do battle against innumera-
ble odds. A few are even faithful to pray regularly for
those who are sent out, and many who remain in the fort
really do hold those "brave, sacrificial" ones in high es-
teem. They roll out the red carpet for them every time
they return to the fort for a visit. But let's face it—where
is the primary interest and effort being put forth? In mov-
ing out to conquer more land or in building a bigger and

better and more comfortable fort? "Hold the Fort" may be a beautiful hymn, but the theology for it never came from the lips of our Commander in Chief. Beloved, let's quit kidding ourselves. Let's quit kidding ourselves about the task before us, the task in which Jesus Christ wants all of us to be involved full-time. There is a new city being prepared for us, there is fire and destruction stored up for this world and all that is in it. Time is running out, and banking hours will soon be over. If you and I are going to take advantage of our God-given opportunities to do any eternal investing, we had better get with it. How much of that in which you are involved or how much of that in which your local church is involved is going to pay off in eternal dividends? Are you focused in on the untold millions that are still untold, or are you primarily focused on the 6 percent at home? The 6 percent are indeed important, but what about the other 94 percent? Are you aware of the opportunities, or have you been kidding yourself?

There are many things here on the home front which disturb and confuse this missionary, and some of those things are the basis for this book—particularly for this chapter. One of those things is a letter I received some years ago from a Christian school training men and women for Christian service. The letter came asking for help in finding vacant pulpits for a new class of graduating seniors. Did I know of any openings? As you may well realize, of course, that letter was intended for former students who were serving in pastorates in the States, but somebody goofed and sent copies to some of us missionaries. Since I received the letter asking for help, I felt that I should do what I could, and I answered it. Certainly, I knew of a number of opportunities—in Japan, in Indonesia, in Brazil, in Africa, in South America, in Taiwan—just to mention a few. Opportunities for men and women. Opportunities for translation work, for evangelism, for church planting. I even guaranteed that the people selected could have an entire city of sixty-five, seventy, or a hundred thousand all to themselves, with no churches on the other side of town sending their buses to take their neighborhood children away. There were opportunities for student work and literature work and camp work—all kinds of opportunities. In fact, I included in my response the fact that we were desperate for help! The original letter had disturbed me when it had arrived, but I was even more disturbed to find that there did not seem to be any interest in the information I sent in response to that letter. As a matter of fact, some people let it be known that the information in my letter of response was not appreciated.

There is another thing that disturbs me. Frequently when I am speaking to Bible school or seminary students about opportunities abroad, I hear someone say, "I could never go out and beg for my support." Can you imagine? People who say that are closing the door to possible service abroad because they find it too difficult to go among the churches and ask for support—or so they say. In the first place, that smacks of building a straw man, for missionaries do not have to beg for support, If they prefer, they do not have to speak of money at all. Does it not seem strange that the very ones who find it so distasteful to go to several churches in search of support for missionary work have no difficulty at all in asking what a church is willing to pay before they can determine if the Lord is leading them to that particular pulpit? I am confused!

But there is something else that disturbs me even more, and that is when a young couple respond to the tremendous opportunities for taking the gospel out to some of the 94 percent out there, when they take the time and personally bear the expense of getting the required years of school, when they follow through on all the necessary red tape of missionary appointment—and then have to spend twelve, eighteen, or even twenty-four months waiting for the Lord's people to come up with the necessary financial support. Somehow, if we could transport that young couple back to the early New Testament church, I have the feeling that some more houses and land would be sold by the believers to raise the necessary funds to get that couple out. But of course, those early believers did not have investment plans for their money, and, with persecution what it was, it was probably better for them to dispose of that property anyway. Nevertheless, I am confused. Where is that majoring in missions emphasis we hear so much about? Where are all those Christians who are so taken up with the question of the Lord's return that they will actually split a church fellowship over the matter of the timing of His return and sometimes even refuse to fellowship with anyone who has a bit different understanding about the eschatological order of events? If they are that excited about the Lord's return, certainly they should jump at the chance to make some quick transfer of deposits from banks here to the Bank of Heaven. If they really believe that the Lord's return is imminent, certainly they would not be too interested in all the material things that will be left behind. Or am I confused here, too? Who is kidding whom?

7

Beloved, Let's Quit Kidding Ourselves

Have you been kidding yourself about missions? Have you been kidding yourself about the outlook, about the reason for missions, about the call, about finances? Have you been kidding yourself about the missionary, his task, his responsibilities, his frailties? Are you really aware of what God is doing in our day and age, and of the fact that He actually wants to involve you somewhere in His great plan and program? Are you really earnestly involved in doing business with the one, five, or ten talents your Lord has entrusted to you, or are you missing out on the opportunities? As a missionary associated with an above-average missionary-minded fellowship of churches and a great host of above-average missionary-minded prayer and financial supporters, I am deeply concerned that most of us are still kidding ourselves about missions. The Lord gives us a beautiful parable in Matthew 13:45-46:

> Again, the kingdom of heaven is like unto a merchant man, seeking goodly pearls: who, when he had found one pearl of great price, went and sold all that he had, and bought it.

That merchant was "pearl minded." When he realized where his fortune lay, he spared no expense, no effort, to lay hold of it. Oh, that God's people today could see the eternal lesson involved here. Actually, the picture is of the Lord Jesus Christ Himself. He considered you and me to be pearls of great price, and He left the glories of heaven to come and purchase us. But more than that, He now offers to you and to me opportunities to invest with Him.

It isn't that Jesus Christ needs our abilities, our help, our material possessions. He is perfectly able to complete His task without us. But He has made it clear that He wants our abilities, our help, our possessions. He wants to show us how to take these things and invest them in such a way that we will reap eternal dividends. The fact of the matter is that you and I really possess nothing. We have simply been put in trust of a few capabilities, a little health, a degree of mental ability, and a few material possessions. These things do not really belong to us. We received them at birth or a short time after and we leave them all when we pass on. The simple truth is that more important than what abilities or possessions we have will be the matter of how we invested them. When Jesus Christ showed him how to invest in eternity, the rich young ruler passed up the opportunity when he considered the price to be too high, and he turned his back on Jesus and walked out of history. A number of poor, uneducated fishermen, on the other hand, left their boats and nets to follow Him, and they made history. Jesus Christ is still looking for men and women who want to make history.

Missionaries around the world are facing opportunities today never before faced by the church of Jesus Christ. The church is growing faster than at any time since Pentecost. In many countries the church is growing so rapidly that missionaries are simply not able to disciple those who are turning to Christ. As a result, many of the cults and heretical offshoots of Christianity are reaping the harvest. Spiritism is growing by leaps and bounds simply because we do not have the forces available to take advantage of the opportunities. Some of you reading this book could very well move out to some of those needy areas, while others of you could be doing far more at the home front to speed them on their way.

The apostle Paul, writing to the Corinthian church, spoke of two motivating forces in his life: (1) the terror of the Lord, and (2) the love of Christ. In 2 Corinthians 5:11 he wrote:

> Knowing therefore the terror of the Lord, we persuade men.

And in verse 14 he said:

> For the love of Christ constraineth us.

In the same way, I find myself writing this book as a result of two motivating forces. On the one hand, I realize the tremendous teaching in the Word of God which deals with the matter of our one day having to stand before the judgment seat of Jesus Christ to give an account of our lives. We read the teaching on the wood, hay, and stubble in 1 Corinthians 3 and we hear the admonition of the Lord in Ezekiel 33:8, where He says to the watchman on the wall:

> When I say unto the wicked, O wicked man, thou shalt surely die; if thou dost not speak to warn the wicked from his way, that wicked man shall die in his iniquity; but *his blood will I require at thine hand* [italics added].

Then, too, there are the parables, which came from the Lord Himself, concerning the day of accounting, and the words He directed to the foolish farmer: "Thou fool!" (Luke 12:20).

Then, on the other hand, there are the many portions of Scripture which speak about God's gracious offers to allow us to share in that which He is doing.

> Verily, verily, I say unto you, He that believeth on me, the works that I do shall he do also; and greater works than these shall he do; because I go unto my Father [John 14:12].

> Ye have not chosen me, but I have chosen you, and ordained you, that ye should go and bring forth fruit, and that your fruit should remain [John 15:16].

Yes, there is the opportunity to make deposits in the Bank of Heaven. I am convinced that a great number in the body of Christ have been kidding themselves about eternal investments. You are perfectly free to use your life the way you desire. You are free to expend your energies in any way you see fit. You can choose your own life occupation and you can use your material possessions exactly as you want to—after taxes, of course. But your accounting days are not over when you have passed inspection by the IRS. There are no statutes of limitation to protect you from misconduct or mismanagement before God's judgment bar. There are eternal rewards to be gained and eternal losses to be suffered, and what you and I are doing with what you and I possess today will determine those losses and those gains. "Be not deceived; God is not mocked" (Gal. 6:7).

God has a special place for you in His overall plan—a place where He can put your abilities, your gifts, your possessions to work for His glory. It is possible that He could use you and your abilities out among the 94 percent, for there are literally thousands of job opportunities on the mission fields of the world for those without theological training. Or it is possible that you are already in the geographical area of His choice for you, but not doing the particular job He has for you. It is even possible that you are in the right spot, doing the right job, but with the wrong motive. It is also possible, as I pointed out earlier, that God has some oil wells He would like to entrust to you, but He is still waiting for you to show Him that you are ready to be trusted with those wells.

Remember, at that final day of accounting, you and I are not going to be judged on the basis of how much we did for Jesus Christ or how much we gave for His work. We are going to be judged on the basis of what portion of our talents and abilities were put to work for Him and what portion of our possessions were invested for Him. What has been done for the praise and recognition of man has already been rewarded by the praise and recognition received. If we gave or if we served to salve our consciences, the salved conscience was the reward. And if our giving was for the purpose of income tax deductions, the income tax deduction was the reward. The Lord has those marked, "Paid in full."

It is my sincere desire that this book will help many to quit kidding themselves about a lot of things.

Moody Press, a ministry of the Moody Bible Institute, is designed for education, evangelization and edification. If we may assist you in knowing more about Christ and the Christian life, please write without obligation to:

Moody Press, c/o MLM, Chicago, Illinois 60610.